Tales From the
Brilliant
Side
of Growing Up
2ND EDITION

To Charles,
FRiend & Fellow
Traveler.
Ray

RAYMOND
KOLCABA

outskirts
press

Outskirts Press, Inc.
http://www.outskirtspress.com

ISBN: 978-1-9772-3998-3

Library of Congress Control Number: 2021907120

PRINTED IN THE UNITED STATES OF AMERICA

This book is dedicated to
Ditch, Stump, Rick, Rodent, Bison, Sam,
Kathy, Chris, Jill, Liz, and my other fellow travelers.
Thank you for bright memories.

Contents

Preface to the Second Edition

A memoir gets interesting with an atypical story. A second edition of a memoir is another matter. I am not only adding novel detail to what most older readers already know about my time and place. As my early time of life recedes, new generations have entered the scene including the coming of age of my grandchildren. The years of my early and middle life are period pieces to the young. They understand the old world's peculiarity contrasted with their current reality. My thirty additional sections give my story more handles to hold onto.

I have stayed within the same boundaries as the first edition, and the mood remains on the bright side of life. Again, I aimed for responses like, "Oh, really?" or "That's unusual.!" The twentieth century was a dark one. Many other writers have covered the grim mood of those times. I peppered my topics with reminders of their dark context if only to provide some contrast for my bright tales. I hope as before that some of my stories, being as factual as memory will permit, bring some lightness to your day.

Introductory

This book is not a tragi-comedy. Many memoirs trend that way. The tragic thread unites the story while the comedic part gives periodic relief. My life has a tragic side, but I avoided it for the most part. I didn't want to dampen the mood too much.

A comic situation stands on its own. It defines its own boundaries. Linkages between situations require a plot. Life is not that way. There is no plot. Incidents in life are like drops falling into a puddle. Each drop makes a splash. The splash is the event that makes for the story. The ripples are the after effects. As they radiate, they join other ripples from other splashes.

My tales are about splashes rather than ripples. Memory of bright events works that way. The splash creates interest while its ripples diminish it. So on with splashes! What holds the stories together? Well, they were part of my early and middle life. Beyond that, I don't think there was a purpose for it all. Let me explain.

As a young child, I held my experiences together with religious glue. I thought that everything happened for a purpose. I told myself little stories. This was what God had in mind because its purpose was so and so. Why did my dad buy gas? God had in mind some moral lesson about minding the gas tank. It would make us more conscientious people. My father benefited morally by buying gas. He served as our good example.

I had enough of this thinking when I questioned inventing purposes. Inventing purposes was too easy. It seemed that I was just making things up. What about events that no one could care about? There seemed to be no rhyme or reason for them. Why did I just blink? Why did I step on the ant? Why do I feel sleepy? Oh, I could make up a purpose to answer these questions. Doing so did not seem honest.

In the whole stupendous universe, most events occur beyond the reach of anyone's eyes or ears. What purposes could they serve? Purposes that only God could know? My questions went on. I eventually grew into thinking that most events did not have a <u>moral</u> purpose. There were just too many events in nature and too few moral purposes that people talked about. I also thought that if we were clever, we could get enough moral purposes out of just a few events. Take George Washington and the cherry tree. We could keep coming up with moral lessons from that one. The gazillions of events in nature are not needed to make whatever is the point.

So, what is the real lesson behind an event? Along with me, you are probably thinking that if there is a real lesson, it is unknowable. We would need to know what God had in mind. For that matter, God could just have wanted my dad to have gas so he could get where he needed to go. Or he may have wanted the shareholders of Texaco to increase their profits. The depths of God's purposes were said to be a mystery. But if we can't plumb these depths, we can't use God's purposes to make sense out of things or to help us make decisions.

Tales have a spotty reputation. It may be a true tale, a stretched one, or a tall tale. We are wary of tales. We think that most are presented as true when they are really stretched or tall. We have psychologists to blame for this. For well over a century, psychologists tried to prove that memory is inaccurate. Study after study showed that when we remember, we don't get things right. It was so much so that it seemed that we could hardly count on memory. But that is no way to live. Life goes much more smoothly when we believe our memory keeps things straight. Just so we are not too far off base.

I am happy thinking that my memories are factual. I think that they are like the memory that the portrait of George Washington is on the dollar bill. Every time I get out a dollar, there is George with his green face and Egyptian haircut. My tales about growing up are like that. I don't need to go back to prove to myself how it was. The psychologists weren't there, so how could they know otherwise? And according to them, their memories are bad too.

I suppose that the events of my growing up have all kinds of purposes. Lord only knows what they are. I am satisfied without much in the name of a purpose if you, the reader, find most of my stories illuminating and on the light side of life. If you find that they brighten your day or charm you in some way. Perhaps they may bring to mind some bright memories of your own.

Chapter I

A Respectable Garage Roof

It didn't all start one day. Life isn't like that. My friend Ditch and I were looking for things to do. He was called Ditch because my uncle George was nicknamed Ditch. As a child uncle George liked to play in mud puddles or so my father said. And my friend was named George, so my brother called him Ditch. His name didn't have anything to do with mud puddles. You get the connection.

Anyway, we were looking for something to do. We were at the silly age. We laughed and laughed over little things. We laughed because we were laughing. We laughed because there was nothing funny. I read comic books, and I liked Donald Duck, Goofy, and Uncle Scrooge. In one comic book, there was a picture of a garage — a regular, freestanding, single garage. It had all sorts of junk on top of it. There was a ladder, an old tire, some paint cans, pieces of wood. You get the picture.

Ditch and I discussed the matter, got out the ladder and looked at his garage roof. We concluded that the roof was not self-respecting. Ah, but we could improve it! We began throwing junk from the garage onto the roof — an old tire, a ladder, an old door, pieces of wood, lawn chairs. We laughed and laughed. We didn't think that anyone would notice the roof because you can't see the roof. The junk was up there out of sight.

Ditch's dad came home from work and was walking up the stairs to the second floor. He glanced out of the window that overlooks the garage roof. His eyes bugged out. He saw the beauty of it all. He ran downstairs asking George what in the world he had done. I don't know how Ditch explained it. I do know that he wasn't laughing. I am glad I wasn't there. The whole comic book thing was my idea. His dad eventually did see some humor in it.

I later realized that many people in the neighborhood could see the garage top from their second story. The newly cluttered garage roof in absence of the comic book explanation could only make neighbors wonder. How in the world did that stuff end up on the garage roof? And so suddenly? As if on purpose?

No Steps on Halloween

Some Russian immigrants lived up the street from Ditch. They were deeply pious Roman Catholics. How these Russians became Roman Catholic I don't know. I thought that Russians were Orthodox Catholic. Anyway, they would go to mass every day. This was unusual. Although some wives went to mass every day, most husbands worked long hours in factories. So did Mr. Stefanov, but he would wake up extra early and attend daily mass before work. Their eldest son was their crowning glory. He was a catholic priest.

On Halloween, we young kids went about trick or treating. The small lots of the houses let even a tiny child visit a number of houses. Each house had a wooden porch with about 5 steps leading up to it. Every Halloween the Stefanovs removed their wooden steps and put them in their garage. They turned out all of their lights and went to bed early.

This prevented trick or treaters from going on their porch and waxing their windows. No treat, so here's a trick. The ghosts, witches, and hobos didn't have a chance to trick the Stefanovs. I thought, "Boy, that is some trick." They weren't supposed to trick us. We were supposed to trick them!

As a young child I wondered about these people. My friends and I thought they were stingy and not good sports. My mother tipped us off that they did not believe in Halloween. I couldn't understand why not. It's only one day a year and children have so much fun. Was there a dark side to Halloween? Was there something to stories about witches and devils? Some older kids did some devilish things. Most of it was petty vandalism like papering parked cars.

The catholic clergy preached against all hallows eve as a pagan day not to be observed by good Catholics. This probably went back to the days when the church competed with pagan faiths for adherents. The Stefanovs were probably not stingy. They were following the teachings of the clergy rather than saving money or not wanting children to have fun. Or so I thought.

Club House and the Rat

My brother and I had a clubhouse made of crate wood. It was my brother's doing, mostly. I was four years younger and followed his lead. The clubhouse was like an igloo. It had a crawl passage for an entrance that then opened up into a central chamber. In the house-part, two of us could sit up without bumping our heads. This whole clubhouse phase was inspired by the Our Gang movies.

Being a member of our club had its privileges. What kid doesn't need a special meeting place for members only? All outsiders would never know what we did in the clubhouse. They would not know what we kept in there. This would make all the kids want to be members of our club. This sounds much like how adults regard their clubs, but that is another matter.

I got a little doctor's bag for Christmas. It had bandages, Mercurochrome, and little bottles of fake medicines. I added bottles. Model airplane glue came in a bottle. They called the glue "dope." It had a strong odor that you weren't supposed to inhale. I put water in an empty glue bottle, but even with the water, you could still smell the glue. One day when playing doctor in the clubhouse, I began treating mosquito bites by taking some cotton and putting some of the glue water on the bite. Lo and behold, it stopped itching! I had found a cure for mosquito bites! At least the itching part.

We had a big cat — named Tommy — who was let out nightly. He liked to sleep in a cardboard box in the clubhouse. One day I crawled through the entry and while on all fours, I could only see an inside corner of the box. I thought that my brother had left a rattail file in the box. I proceeded and as my head loomed over the box, I saw a foot-long rat. I shot out of the entryway. With my heart pounding, I slowly realized that the rat was dead. Our Tomcat had taken his kill back to his nest. The memory of encountering the rat still gives me shivers.

Inch of the Klondike

A Quaker breakfast cereal advertised a deed for a square inch of Yukon Land. Two box tops and 25 cents or some such thing. They used all the romance of the gold rush, Klondike, and miners. I sent in my box tops for my inch of real land. My inch may have gold on it! I may be rich! As a boy, I liked owning property. I intended to visit my plot in the Yukon some day.

I got my deed. It was big, handsome, and official looking. My plot number was on it. I hid it away in a safe place. The years passed. I thought that someone would eventually contact me about my land. Someone would want to collect taxes or buy me out or notify me that such and such will be done unless I do whatever. I received no letter. I thought long and hard about my square inch. Was it right up against other parcels on all 4 sides? Could I gain access to my land? If I dug for gold, would I probably have ruined a lot of adjacent property?

The inch isn't much on the Earth's surface, but it goes a long way down into the Earth. The Earth is a sphere, and my inch projected down to Earth's core as a pyramid. How far down does it go before it disappears for all practical purposes? Do I own a ton of soil and rock, 10 tons, or what? I often thought that my inch may be under water or may be sitting on an inaccessible mountainside. Did they take care to assure that every inch was good flat prospecting land? Or did they just buy a few acres for a song and sell off inches? Maybe they never even visited the land — a bunch of cereal executives sitting around a table in Michigan.

The last time I saw the deed, I recall that I noticed it was not hand signed. Some signatures were reproduced to make it look real to a kid, but it lacked legality. I don't know if I threw it away at that time. But every now and then when I am looking through some boxes of old things, my inch of Klondike comes to mind. Maybe this time I will find my deed. If I did, I probably would do nothing. But somewhere, there in a vault of the cereal company, my name is affixed to a ledger, along with thousands of other kids from the 1950's, who own those inches and dreams.

Bath Tub Treasure Hunting

We liked to play pirates and I went through my pirate phase. I was obsessed with being a pirate, brandishing flintlock pistols, dressing like a pirate, talking like one — Arrrr Matey! I memorized the opening of Treasure Island, "From sailors' tales to sailors' tombs. . . ." I was transfixed by Burt Lancaster's speech at the beginning of the movie The Crimson Pirate — it's a pirate land and a pirate world! Pirates were after treasure, and the bottom of the ocean was just littered with sunken ships most of which had chests filled with treasure.

I recall that that picture was put into a vivid image in a Walt Disney comic book. You just dive beneath the surface of the ocean and there is another world populated by colorful fish and sunken galleon after sunken galleon. All we needed was one treasure to be on easy street and all those treasures were ripe for the picking on the ocean floor. I had an idea! Drain the ocean and then we could walk out pick up all the treasures.

"How could this be done?" you ask. I thought that everyone in the world should be asked to fill their bath tubs at the same time. This would drain the oceans. I thought that the problem with the idea was that we couldn't get everyone to cooperate in filling their tubs at the same time. But suppose we could. I thought that whoever found treasure would cut me in on the take since my bathtub idea made it all possible.

I asked my dad about it. He said that there were not enough bath-tubs to drain the oceans.

Cooper's Warmth

At recess in kindergarten, Larry grabbed my hat and ran with it. I was surprised. I instinctively ran after him. He was laughing. I managed to grab my hat, but he wouldn't let go of it. I punched him, and we began to fight. Then big hands from some big adult grabbed both of us. It was Mrs. Moser. She was the assistant principle — the school enforcer, the muscle behind the rules. She was tall, portly, with gray hair. She was much feared. It wasn't because of what she did. It was because of the way she looked.

Ms. Cooper was my kindergarten teacher. As class began after recess, she had Larry and me stand before the class. She gave us the business for fighting. She said that we were wrong to fight. I didn't like what I was hearing. I was the wronged party. Tell the class about how Larry stole my cap and wouldn't give it back. Before I could accuse Larry, Ms. Cooper put her arms around me and drew me to her bosom. I felt her warm body and was comforted that everything was all right. I kept quiet and enjoyed being there.

The First Apple of My Eye

I was five and in kindergarten. Parents were invited to watch us do various kindergarten things such as skipping to music. There was a girl in the class named Margie. I enjoyed looking at her. I think she enjoyed being with me. We smiled a lot at each other. We joined hands and skipped together to the music. The music was an upbeat tune like A Tisket, A Tasket, A Green and Yellow Basket. It had a dynamite second part that let us really dig into vigorous skipping. She had this neat dress with a flouncy skirt. We bounced along at a brisk pace. This made me feel good. We skipped with gusto. Margie's mom was talking to my mom. They were smiling about what a cute pair we were. I didn't care about that. I liked Margie. After the kindergarten year, her family moved out of the school district. I never saw her again.

Safe Crossing

My first-grade teacher asked our class, "When is it safest to cross the street?" She expected an answer like, "When the light is red." I replied, "When the light is green and no cars are coming, it is safest to cross. Cars going the other way are stopped for the red light." This was way before the time when you could turn right on red. Mrs. Simpson did not know what to say. She just started talking about waiting until the light turns red.

The Ice Man

We hung a cardboard sign in the dining room window that said, "Ice." This told the iceman to stop and deliver a block of ice. He would park on the street. He would grab a block of ice with ice calipers. The block was about a foot on each side. He wore a sheet of leather over his shoulder on which he would place the ice block all the while holding onto it with the calipers. It looked heavy and cold.

Our icebox was in the kitchen. When we opened the door, we saw a compartment on top with a door. It was sort of like where a freezer would be when they were inside a single door refrigerator. A drain tube ran from the ice compartment to the bottom of the icebox. The melt water went into a pan. As the ice melted, we needed to empty the pan periodically. It took the ice block several days to melt. When we missed the iceman, we drove to an icehouse and bought a block. This was where the iceman got his ice for delivery. My Dad had ice calipers in his tool chest. During the icebox era, ice calipers were a common tool.

The Clothes Prop and the Plum Tree

My brother was mischievous. He knew how to push my mother's buttons. She would get angry with him for something or another. He would sass her, and then run. We had a dining room table that was round. She would chase him around the table. Around and around they would go. All the while he would be laughing — until she caught up with him.

Sometimes he would run outside and she would chase him. He would climb the plum tree. He would mock her. She would get a clothes prop and swing away at him in the tree. He would come down to the point where she would just miss him with the prop. As she would swing from her tiptoes and miss, he would laugh and laugh. This made her all the more angry. One time after she missed many times and was fatigued, she began to laugh too.

His other trick would just drive my mother crazy. He would run around the house and then collapse. He would pretend that he was dead. He would hold his breath to pretend that he had stopped breathing. He scared the dickens out of her. After she realized that he was faking and he started to laugh at her again, she really let into him. That time she really spanked him. Her usual response to naughtiness, though, was to say the dreaded words, "Wait until your father comes home!"

My poor dad would be exhausted after a day of labor in the steel mill. The last thing he wanted to do was beat the kids. He wanted to be greeted, appreciated, drink a beer, and talk about the day. His happy smile would turn to that ashen look when my mother told him about the mischief and the need for corporal punishment. We had a leather strap with tails cut in its end. It was hanging by the basement steps. As the younger child, I saw what happened to my brother. I usually obeyed my parents to avoid the strap. The swats he got taught me the lesson.

Lone Ranger Break Out

Another kind of corporal punishment was to be locked in the basement. Isolation was supposed to lead to reflection. Our basement door had a skeleton key lock. The key was always in the lock on the kitchen side of the door. After being locked in, we would sit on top of the steps and wait to be released. My brother saw the Lone Ranger escape from a locked room. He knocked the key off a peg onto a piece of paper and then pulled the paper under the door.

My brother just couldn't wait to try the tactic to escape from the basement. He pulled a pointless prank just to be locked in the basement. My parents detected that something was amiss. The prank seemed half-hearted. It was as if it was part of a larger plan. They were right. As he was locked in the basement, he had a piece of newspaper in hand. My parents usually sat around the kitchen table and talked after dinner. They were interrupted by a rustling sound of the newspaper coming under the door. My brother took a piece of wire and poked the key out of the keyhole so that it fell on the paper. He pulled the key under the door and unlocked it. The noise of it all drew my parents' attention. My parents were amused and just let things return to normal.

The Steps Hill

My tricycle was a hand-me-down from my brother. When he got a big one, I got the small one. I dreamed of going faster and faster. As a child of four, my mother let me ride around the driveway in the back yard. She could carry on with her chores without watching me all of the time. I got the idea that I could go really fast by riding down a hill. The back porch steps, five in number, seemed like a good hill. I figured that I would be going so fast that I would move down the steps like going down a smooth hill. I hauled the tricycle to the landing at the top. I got on and pushed off. I remember hitting the first step and then no more. The trike flipped and I landed on my head. My mother heard the noise and ran out to save me. I had quite a bump on my head. I still didn't know why it wasn't like a hill. I didn't try it again.

Puddle Under Ditch

I was probably three and Ditch was just about two. We were playing in my yard. We were both in a crouch position. It was spring and Ditch had shorts on. As we were playing, a puddle appeared under Ditch. I saw it form slowly, and in a great delayed reaction, he began to cry. His crying started with facial expression and built and grew into a loud cry. He ran home. I hardly realized what had happened. I asked my mom about it. She said that he couldn't control his pee and then became wet and disturbed. I worried for Ditch the next time I saw him.

The Lumber Jack and the Poplar Tree

I was about eight or nine years old. I saw some TV shows about the romance of being a lumberjack. Hearty men. Manly men. Joyous men who express enthusiasm. They mostly speak with a French accent with names like Pierre. They work hard and eat a lot, usually stacks of pancakes with much syrup. They are admired by all for their courage and strength and pure physical vitality. Chop the tree. Shout, "Timber!"

With the world of lumber jacking alive within me, I goaded my father into cutting down a thirty-foot poplar tree growing at our backyard fence. He resisted. He was not drawn to be a lumberjack. He didn't see that lumber jacking was necessary for having a reason to wake up in the morning. But, after enough begging, he agreed. We had an ax. He set to work chopping the tree down. I was not quite of ax age. But I enjoyed being in on the action — of seeing the tree fall.

The tree came down. After the tree fell, I began to feel sad. The mighty tree was gone. My heart sank. It was alive a few moments ago, and now it was dead. There was just a space by our backyard fence. All that remained was a stump. It no longer seemed romantic nor manly to cut down trees just for being a lumberjack. We did not need to cut down the poplar tree.

Say "Celery"

The three-colored plastic torpedo bomber was diving on its prey. The sliding cockpit window let the gunner take care of enemy fighters. At four, I played with my brother's toy. I zipped around the bedroom making airplane sounds. My brother saw me with his plane and took it away from me. "Mom! He's going to break it." I cried and went into a rage. I hit him. My mother tried to keep the peace. "Say you are sorry Raymond." I pouted, and said, "I am not going to say celery." "You must say you are sorry for hitting him." "You can't make me say celery." She wanted me to say celery and I was not going to do it — twist my arm as she may. Mom thought I was just being stubborn.

My Doll

While my brother was in school, my mother took me to a busy shopping area called Broadway and 55th. We walked about half a mile to the bus. The trolley bus ride was about twenty minutes. The area was noted for its five and ten cent stores. Kresgees was the largest. The lure for me was another lead soldier for my collection. On one such trip, I passed a doll. Immediately I wanted it. I still remember the vision of it standing up high on top of some boxes. I was attracted to its clothes and how neat it looked. My mother said that dolls were for girls. She said that she would not buy the doll. I started to cry.

That evening mom discussed my heartrending response with my father. They agreed that I should get the doll. We went back a week later and bought the boy doll. I played with the doll and enjoyed moving its arms and legs, watching its eyes roll back in its head as I laid it down. I dressed it and undressed it. I had a deep need for that doll. My attraction to the doll played itself out. After it was broken, I had no desire for another doll.

Organic Comforts

About age four, our family went to nearby park. There was a gully, a grassy hillside, and grassy nooks to lie in. I made contact with the grass and rolled. I rolled down the hill again and again. I assumed a fetal position in a curve in the gully. I nestled in an indentation in the grass. Much time passed. I was absorbed in these activities. All the while I muttered sounds of fulfillment, and I remember being wholly happy and satisfied. The singular joy of these experiences stands out to me today. Almost all of this made no sense to my parents. To that point in my life, I don't think I had made contact with the smell and freshness of the grass and earth. I had a deep need to do so.

No Memory, No me

In the mist that settles the mind with sleepiness, I remembered what my parents were talking about just before bedtime. They were talking about World War Two. I tried to remember the war. No matter how hard I tried, I could not remember the war. It came to me that I was not there then. It was before there was a me. I thought that I must have entered life after the war. I realized that I had a beginning.

This was puzzling. It seemed to me that I was always here. The present did not have a beginning. I tried to imagine not being here. I could not. It must be that I always existed. But it was true that I was not present for World War Two. I had a beginning. This was strange. No me, but always here.

A few nights later in the ephemeral twilight before sleep, I thought about the distant future. Years from now, I would be. Would there be a time when I would be no more? I didn't know. It seemed like I would live forever. The present doesn't stop. I brought back my memory of not being alive during World War Two. If there was a time before I was here, there could be a time after which I was here. I became afraid. I thought about death.

Focee Man

Our house was buttoned down tight as a drum. I was not in school yet. All the men in the neighborhood were at work during the day. Most women were housewives. Many women had pre-school age children like my mom. There was little crime in the neighborhood, but everyone was wary of new faces and intruders. One day an old man with a long and bushy white beard knocked on our back door. Through a locked door, my mother told him to go away. He asked for food or soup. My mother again told him to go away. He was angry that my mother turned him down. She said that the focee man (bearded man) didn't deserve a handout. I think that he was a hobo. I could tell that my mother was worried that if she let him in, he might do us harm.

Nicking the Faucet Handle

I hated being called "cute." I hated it when mom said, "Look at him, isn't he cute." I was always embarrassed. I didn't know what they saw. I didn't think that it had anything to do with me. I felt like an object on display. I didn't want to be an object on display. I usually got angry, sometimes having a red face. Mom didn't understand my reaction. She thought that my response made me all the more cute. As the younger brother, I was the "baby" of the family. As the years passed, I resented being called the baby too. All through my teen years I was still called the baby of the family. After reaching adulthood, I finally didn't mind being referred to as the baby.

One blistering hot August day, the house was like an oven. We had no fan. The windows were open, but the air didn't move. I was down to my underwear. I had a long tee shirt on. We were all in the kitchen. I began to act silly. I started dancing. My parents thought it was cute. I began whirling while straightening my arms with the bottom of the tee shirt in my hands. I turned in circles until I fell down. I hit my head and bawled. I had a goose egg on my head.

My parents didn't like fetching me things. They complained about it. I didn't like relying on them for things. I thought to myself, "I don't need them." I wanted a glass of water. I was too short to reach the faucet. They were criticizing me for not getting my own water. I decided to show them. I put the footstool in front of the sink. I got up on it. I reached up on my tiptoes. With a long stretch, my forefinger nicked the faucet handle. I did it again and again until the faucet was open. I got my glass of water. They seemed pleased. I think they liked my determination. I wasn't trying to prove anything. I wanted to get the water myself because I was angry. I was angry because of their unwillingness to help me.

Wagon Trains

TV westerns gave inspiration for play. We played wagon train. We were pioneers going out west. We were challenged by Indians, outlaws, and terrible weather. We would wire together three or four of our play wagons. One of us, usually Rick, would be the horse. The little kids would sit in the wagons. The wagons contained all of our supplies, guns, and ammunition. The wagon train would move up the sidewalk around to the next block, down the street behind ours, and back around the block to the starting point.

Along the way someone would shout, "Indians!" We would grab our guns, tip over the wagons, and fire away until the trouble passed. We would right the wagons, and put everything back in them. The little kids would get back in. Rick, our horse, would proceed until the next attack by outlaws. "Got one. Got another one!" We would do this for hours.

Coal Furnace

Dad would drive to the railroad tracks to order five tons of coal from the Pocahontas Coal Company. The delivery guy would shovel the five tons into our coal bin — a room in our basement for storing coal. The coal would last most of a winter. In the dead of winter, my dad would add a lump of coal to the fire in the furnace and then go to bed. The lump would last two or three hours. The house would chill down. In the middle of the night when the house was mighty cold, my mother would go down stairs and put on another lump.

Our bedroom had a single register. Even with the lump burning, little heat would make its way up to the second floor. The furnace had no fan. Warm air rises, right? If you touched the register in our room, it would be barely warm. Needless to say, when we got out of bed in the morning, the room was frigid. My brother and I would run down stairs shivering and with goose bumps. We would sit next to the oven. My mother lit the oven in the morning to warm the kitchen. It was hard to leave the oven for the cold kitchen table where breakfast was served. One reason I enjoyed elementary school was that it had robust steam heat. I had a chance to shake the chills, but the steam heat and florescent lights made me groggy.

Ash Cans

Besides our garbage can, we had two others. One of them took cans and bottles. Another was for ashes. The coal furnace left cinders and ashes. It had to be cleaned out periodically. My father got his ash cans from work. They were made of heavy steel. The first time I saw black people was on trash collection day. At that time the trash men went into your back yard, used a kind of grappling hook to hoist the cans onto a dolly with metal wheels. They used the hook to pull the dolly to the street.

I remember they wore long black coats. They walked fast. Their appearance was striking and beautiful. They always seemed to be happy, talking and laughing with each other. At that time, we had no black people living in the neighborhood. The black men seemed exotic and interesting.

"Hopalong Cassidy"

Ditch's parents were the first on the street to have a TV. All of us young kids were invited to watch a program. We sat on the floor in a row of five staring at the TV. The show was Hopalong Cassidy. It was amazing. It was like a movie in the living room. We did not want the show to end. Later my brother said that Hopalong Cassidy was once called "Runalong" Cassidy. He fell off of his horse and had to have his leg amputated. He got a wooden leg, so he had to change his name to Hopalong.

Chapter II

The Safety Official

When in sixth grade, I was asked by my favorite teacher — Mr. Nolt — to be a crossing guard. I got to wear the armband informing everyone that I was an official safety guard. I used the safety flag. I held it to restrain the younger kids until it was safe to cross the street. After danger passed, I would move the flag parallel to the cross walk and everyone could then cross under my watchful eye. I took myself to be one of the best crossing guards that Mr. Nolt had.

The first week was an eye opener. Certain parents who walked their children to school acted like they didn't need a crossing guard. I would have my flag in the restrain position, and they would walk around it! One mother even pushed it aside. They weren't supposed to do that. Like everyone else they were supposed to wait for my sign of all clear. When they disregarded my lead, some other kids crossed with them. I felt challenged.

I talked to Mr. Nolt about the problem. He had to come and inform the delinquent parents of what they were supposed to do. They couldn't just disregard the rules. I was a crossing guard, after all, to be respected. I knew when it was safe to cross. They had no right to cross on their own because the corner was manned by a guard. Mr. Nolt minimized their actions and explained that they didn't have to wait for my "all clear." I asked him what I was doing there if I couldn't make sure that safety was first? He said that there was nothing he could do. I quit my position as crossing guard.

The Moon is Going to Fall from the Sky

On a starry night, I was at uncle Butch's in the yard looking up at the night sky. I hadn't stared at the night sky that intensely before. My dad and his brothers were talking about flying saucers and all that is mysterious and unknown. After seeing many science fiction movies, I knew what they were talking about. This was the nineteen fifties. As I fixated on the moon, I noticed that the moon moved. It jiggled. Sometimes it moved a lot. After a while, I saw it bouncing all over the place. I tried not to look at it.

When we got home, I told my dad that the moon was moving around. Something was wrong with it. My dad said that it was going to be o.k. The moon had been up there for a very long time. My brother said that it was probably clouds moving in front of the moon that made it seem to move. I didn't believe him. I went outside and looked for clouds. The night seemed cloudless. Nothing was moving in front of the moon. But the moon, ah, it was moving around and bouncing more than ever. I worried that I was alone in realizing that something fatal was happening to the moon. I decided not to look. I went to bed hoping that the moon would be there the next night. It was.

House Blessing

It was a yearly event. The priest would come to bless the house. He would sweep in chanting a prayer, in his vestments, sprinkling holy water. The cantor would usually be with him singing. We were a working-class family and the parish was mostly working-class. The priest was always asking for money. The first service on Sunday was in Old Church Slavonic. I didn't understand what was being said. Week after week and year after year I stood there not making sense out of what was going on.

One part of the service, however, was in English — when he asked for donations. Usually, the end of the sermon involved the part about money. I understood him very well. He was always trying to shame the congregation into giving more money. Sometimes there were three collections! The church bulletin would publish the names of all parishioners with the amount they donated next to their names.

So, it would be reasonable to think that the blessing of the house would be tied to money. My mother commented that the priest always went into every room, even every closet, to see if you had anything new. He would spy and assess how high you were living. New furniture, a TV, or new appliances would signal that you were holding out. The church wanted its share. I took away a lesson. We had to pray to God to protect us from the priest.

Zorro

I went through my Zorro phase. Once the Disney movie came out, my life changed. I made a mask. I used a broom handle or a tree branch as my sword. I jumped from sofa to chair. I slashed a Z in the air. I got a red crayon. I put Z's on every surface that Mom would let me draw on. The masked hero was all over the house. The sign proved that he was there. This surprised his nobleman enemies. How could the elusive Zorro get by the guards?

Flies

When I was about ten with little to do on a blistering July day, I thought that I would rid the yard of flies. They were always around our garbage can. They would land on the hot concrete of our driveway and sun themselves. There appeared to be a dozen of them — three or four on the drive and perhaps another eight or so near the can. After swatting the flies on the drive with a fly swatter, others took their place and were swatted too. Soon others took their place on the drive, and after swatting them the same thing occurred. Others replaced them.

At first, I thought that I had greatly underestimated the number of flies on our property. As the dead flies grew into piles, I realized that flies must be coming in from all over the neighborhood. The new flies were feeding on the old dead flies. After two hours of this activity, I had a large number of piles with dozens of flies in each. I had trouble keeping up with the plague of flies that in one-by-one fashion appeared on the piles. We were talking many hundreds of flies.

I thought that the number of flies must be limited and that I had a chance of ridding the neighborhood of flies. But with hundreds of dead flies on the drive and more appearing almost immediately, I had no idea what that number would be. The piles reeked of the peculiar smell of dead flies. Finally, my father asked me to quit and he washed the flies from the drive with a garden hose. Once the stench was gone, few new flies arrived to feed on the corpses in the grass.

I was never sure if a dead fly attracted the new flies or if each fly had a territory marked out where when one died, others would expand their territory by moving into it. The latter hunch seemed unlikely because the sheer number of flies indicated that they were drawn from quite a distance. But, could the smell even carry that far? Perhaps it was a combination of scent along with flies moving into a number of vacated territories and finally picking up the scent that drove them to their carrion.

Bu Cabbage on the Horezon

I always thought that I was not in the know. Older kids always seemed to know what was what. A simple example comes to mind. I walked into the cafeteria of the middle school to eat the bag lunch I brought from home. I went into the cafeteria line to buy some milk, and I saw that the menu board listed "bu cabbage." For quite a number of days I sort of saw it but it didn't register. Then one day I wondered, "What in the world is 'bu cabbage'?" I asked Tom, my buddy, and he didn't know. "It's a kind of cabbage, isn't it Tom?" "I don't know Ray." "Like green cabbage or red cabbage?" Finally, when I got home, I asked mom. "What is boo cabbage?" She said, "How to you spell it?" I said, "bu." She said, "Oh, that's buttered cabbage." Of course.

The next day I brought up bu cabbage to my friend Paul in home-room. He thought that I was a know-it-all. I explained that I didn't figure it out. I asked mom. He then said that he saw the movie "Lost HOR-e-ZON." I said, "No. the word is ho-RI-zon." He said that I was obviously wrong and that he would ask about it and prove it to me. I was pretty sure that it was not HOR-e-ZON.

Fiction is Not True

When in seventh grade, you couldn't ask me what something was all about. I admitted that I didn't know much. I began reading science books. I thought that fiction was of no use because it was not true. You don't have to know much to make up stories. You only need to be clever. Liars seem to have good stories until confronted with facts. I thought that fiction is written by lazy people. They didn't make the effort to find the facts.

My English teacher, Mrs. Heiman, did not agree with me. She tried to get me to read fiction written for my age. I did not want to know about some fictitious kid who played baseball whose team eventually won the championship. There was no kid and no championship. She said that fiction was fun and entertaining. It was not fun for me. I told her that it seemed to be a waste of time. We could better use the time to learn something — something in a science book.

Anyway, I started reading science books. But on every subject, there was a limit to the amount of information, say on planets, in middle school science books. The more books I read on planets, the more I would see that they repeated the same information. It was hard to find books that said more.

When the space race began with Sputnik, I wrote away to compa-nies that made rockets, like Raytheon and Northrop Grumman. They sent back neat pictures of rockets and interesting material with more information than I could find in the science books. A nice chunk of it, however, was in concepts and language that I didn't understand. I had no familiarity with graphs and little with mathematics. I did not know what they were talking about.

As a young kid I was forever trying to catch up. But no matter what they told me and no matter how much I learned, I was always facing the fact that little was clear to me. I was just looking for basic information. I now have enough basic information for making my way through the part of the world familiar to me. Nonetheless I still feel that I am playing catch up. After a while seeking answers to practical questions is tiring.

A Young Tom Edison

Another interest I developed at the time was electronics. My brother had taken a shop course in electronics and from him I learned about vacuum tubes, radios, and transformers. Alan Kovach was a fellow student in seventh grade science and something of an electronics genius. The courses, teachers, and library at the junior high school had almost nothing to offer Alan. I spent some time with him. His family lived in a factory neighborhood near The Beltline Railroad. Their house was sandwiched between two small factories. There were not many other kids around. He hung out with his older brother and experimented with electronics.

Alan built radios and other electronic devices. I read Popular Science magazine and did some of their projects. For a science project I made a Tesla coil, and for another, a simple hydroelectric plant. Together we designed a multistage rocket with a satellite payload. When it came to the sort of propellant we should use, Alan said it had to be liquid fuel or the rocket would not reach Earth orbit. Besides catalogs for pumps and valves, we couldn't find where to buy liquid oxygen. We discussed how it would be shipped. We concluded that we couldn't get it through the mail. Besides, even if we could somehow get it delivered, we had no place to store it. We decided not to try to launch a satellite.

Alan explained much about what worked and what didn't. He was a hands-on kind of guy. I liked visiting his basement where he always had some interesting project going. When I found a new project in Popular Science, Alan would explain it to me in language I could understand.

In science class, he was very quiet and shy. Our science teacher had no idea that Alan was way beyond the curriculum and apparently way beyond her. When we asked questions, she didn't begin to know where to find answers. Of course, neither did we. That's why we were asking her.

During the early years of schooling, we were all subjected to batteries of standardized tests. Alan was tested and classified as average. In high school, he was put into a lower track than me. I sometimes wonder what became of him. He was a young Thomas Edison when I knew him.

Seasoned Water

Joel had guppies. He had some baby guppies. He gave me a pair. That started my hobby of keeping tropical fish. By junior high school, I had a metal rack in the dining room with four aquariums. It was an ugly rack. It was not a piece of furniture. My mother liked the fish. She did not complain about the industrial appearance of the set up.

At times I let the tanks go too long without cleaning them. Mom never complained. One summer day, I noticed hundreds of jiggling things swimming in a tank. They were going up and down. I studied them with hard eyes with my heart pounding. They looked strange. They were strange. I worried what alien life was hatching in my tank. The next morning, I saw two mosquitoes sitting on top of the water. I panicked. I quickly put soap in the water. If I had waited longer, we would have had a house full of mosquitoes.

I was at the point in my hobby where my angelfish kept dying. Everyone liked angelfish. They were large and flat in the shape of a triangle balanced on one of its points. They were graceful with interesting stripes. I tried to figure out what was going wrong. The little book on angelfish said that I should start with seasoned aquarium water. I always took tap water and put some anti-chlorine drops in it. I asked my friend Ron if that was seasoned water. He said that he didn't think so. He said that he never bought any seasoned water for his tanks. But he didn't have any angelfish.

There was a pet store a bus ride away. We liked to go there to buy new fish. I was always excited to get new fish. The store had about forty tanks with fish in them. Ron and I thought that they had to have seasoned water. The owner of the store was a short heavy guy. His gut hung over his belt. He always wore T-shirts that were too short. Part of his belly was always bare for all to see. His family lived behind the shop. His kids were often in the store helping out or some such thing. He smoked cigars. One side of his mouth was always turned up — the side with the cigar. If one wasn't lit, he would chew on the unlit butt. Somehow it always smelled worse than a lit one. He usually had a scraggly beard. He was quite a sight.

When on the bus, Ron wondered how we were going to get the water home. How could we carry five or ten gallons of it back on the bus? I told him that we could worry about it later. Besides, they had to help you get it out of the store. Otherwise, people wouldn't buy their water.

We went up to the counter. I explained to the guy that I was reading the little book on angelfish. It said that you were supposed to start with seasoned water. I asked if he had any. He looked puzzled. "What kind of water?" he asked. I said, "You know, aquarium water." He looked out at all of his tanks. "I could give you some water from the tanks." I said, "It has to be special seasoned water." He said, "Once the fish are in a tank for a while, the water becomes seasoned." I began to get the picture. Old aquarium water was seasoned water. The fish season the water with their excretions.

Fire Drill

Like clockwork, we had fire drills. Every month or two, the fire alarm would ring. The junior high school would empty out. We would get the "all clear" and go back in. There was always low morale during a fire drill. We were supposed to act like it was real when we knew that it wasn't. Then there was the prank pulling of the fire alarm. We usually did not get very far before we were called back to class. One day the alarm rang, and the school emptied. Hundreds of us lined the boulevard in front of the school.

The last teacher to exit with her class was Mrs. Fox. She had this thinning hair that stuck up giving her an electric look, like she had just been shocked. She was short, about fifty, and had that distant look in her eyes that indicated that she was not all there. I think that the students (one teacher called us "hellions") had gotten the better of her over the years. Rumor had it that once she had trouble controlling a class. She broke down and said, "If you don't be quiet, I am going to jump out of the window." The class chanted back, "Go ahead!" A story like that was passed around to new students. This didn't increase Mrs. Fox's chances of controlling new classes. Some of the hellions took it as a challenge to get Mrs. Fox to threaten to jump out of the window again.

Mrs. Fox had had enough of the fire drill. She led her class back into the building. Moments later, she came running out of the building ahead of her class with smoke rising from her frizzy hair. She was in a panic. Moments later, fire engines roared up the boulevard. As the sirens blared and the firetrucks began to appear, this enormous and spontaneous cheer rose from the students on the sidewalk. The cheer was so loud and affirmative that it brought tears to your eyes. The building was on fire.

Our school had a section of students who were slow learners. Probably today we would say they were developmentally disabled or learning challenged. Officially they were called "special students." The student body called them "specials." I suppose they were called that because they were not in the mainstream classes. Some students in this group were more than seventeen years old. To us, many of them looked like men. We were all thirteen to fifteen. Anyway, one special student set the auditorium stage curtains on fire. He didn't like the school and was acting out. The fire was quickly put out. Apart from the smell of smoke, we continued with the school day.

The Library

From childhood on, I enjoyed libraries—- the look and smell of them. You got a sense that there was a solemn and serious purpose behind them—- sort of like church. My mother took me to the local library when I was a small kid.

Our middle school library had age-appropriate books. With American History, for example, you got the impression that only giants were part of the American story. Foreigners were invaders like the British or autocratic like the Spanish. I bought into it and enjoyed reading the exploits of John Paul Jones, Ethan Allen and The Green Mountain Boys, Andy Jackson and Jean Lafitte. I thought that the exploits of these heroes were true. Later, with some anger, I learned that the lives of my heroes were by and large just good stories.

Many of the boys at Nathan Hale Junior High School made a point of disregarding school. The neighborhood was working class. At the time, boys could legally quit school at age sixteen. Some of them were just marking time until they could go to work. Some of them had nothing to lose by upsetting order in the school. Other boys and girls went to trade schools instead of high school. Many of them did not care about ordinary academics. Needless to say, student attitudes were often anti-institution.

For some, the library was where you caught a few winks. My friend Mike took a thick dictionary, hollowed it out with a razor blade, and put in a transistor radio. That way when he pretended to sleep in the library or in study hall, with his head on his desk, he could listen to rock and roll on the radio.

Other boys would bring broken saw blades from wood shop, insert them under their library table and twang them. When they did this, the quiet of the place would be interrupted with a twang, twang. Of course, the perpetrator looked innocent like everyone else. Every time, the librarian, Miss Ludke, either perked up or pretended not to hear the twang. She was young and very kind. You could tell that her aim was not to show anger. Then she would be jarred with another twang. The kids were trying to get a rise out of her but she usually wouldn't cooperate. Kids, as always, knew she was trying to hold it back. That was part of the fun.

As school legend had it, a saw blade was left sticking out under a table and some innocent kid jammed his leg into it. It was like a fishhook caught in his leg. When he tried to get up, he couldn't because the teeth of the blade were holding him. He was attached to the table and bleeding profusely. The legend had it that in the end, he survived.

In the spring and fall, the worst of it was when the library windows were open. There was no air conditioning in the school so relief from hot weather required opening windows. Sometimes "students" would tie heavy books to the window shade cords and throw them out of the window. This would unravel the shade down the side of the building.

Another prank was to throw books out the window onto the front lawn. This would be done in a sneaky way. As a student would walk by an open window, he would fling a book out while nonchalantly checking out the librarian to make sure she was not looking. At the end of the day, poor Miss Ludke would go down from the third-floor and collect books from the front lawn.

I didn't participate in the mischief. I liked the library and Miss Ludke. As a library, however, it came up short. Even I, as a naïve and uninformed twelve and then thirteen-year-old, had trouble finding books on my interests. Besides American history books and terrible age-appropriate fiction, the library's only saving grace was the encyclopedias. I didn't understand most of what I encountered in the <u>Britannica</u>; <u>World Book</u> was more in line with my abilities. Even the encyclopedias were quite empty of the topics that made me want to read—— articles about science generally, the space race with the Russians, and rockets.

The Encyclopedist

I got absorbed in eighth grade history. Old Mr. Matson, our history teacher, showed a liking for the subject. He would always deliberately say, "George **War**shington." I thought that it must have had something to do with Washington being a general. No one asked him why he pronounced the name that way. But he always emphasized the War part of "**War**shington." I liked Matson's class and decided to study hard to earn an A. I gave extra reports. For doing so, I was ridiculed and tormented by some of the tough guys in the class. I loved American history anyway.

I found my information for reports in <u>Worldbook Encyclopedia</u>. I started to read the encyclopedia widely. Matson sold World Book on the side and came to visit my parents. He probably said some flattering things about me and then talked about how having a World Book set in the home would make me flower. My parents were polite but would have none of it. I begged a bit, but they said that we did not need an encyclopedia. My mother said that it would collect dust. I suspected that the real reason was that my parents did not want to spend their money that way.

I decided to not let them hold me back. I would read the encyclopedia in the school library, and at home I would gather my own encyclopedia. I took two drawers of a dresser in the dining room, wrote the alphabet on separators, and put entries on pieces of stiff paper and cardboard. I used paste to mount the articles. I went through magazines and newspapers. I cut out articles on any topic that I wanted to remember. I realized that most of what I read, I would forget. The encyclopedia would store my knowledge. I could return to it whenever I wished.

My encyclopedia did not have most of what was in World Book. I thought that if I kept at it long enough, I would have something on most topics. I filled the two drawers. I had hundreds of entries. After my interest in the encyclopedia waned, it remained in the drawers for some years unused. I was not drawn to recover my knowledge. I forgot most of what was there. When it came time for me to clean out the drawers, a demand from Mom, I went through the material. I looked at the entries before throwing them out — one by one.

The Banging Trash Can Lid

The neighbor kid Billy begged endlessly for a dog. His parents had an active social life and were away from home much of the time. My parents knew that a dog would be left alone for long stretches of time. Billy got his wish. The neighbors decided to tie the dog behind the garage, and when they walked away, it barked a lot. The dog had a good disposition. It was some kind of wirehair. Usually, it stopped barking fairly soon. When our neighbors did not come home for a while, the dog let loose with a mournful bark and howl. We felt sorry for the dog.

We don't know exactly what happened. All of a sudden there was pandemonium with the dog wailing and running up and down the front lawns. Its leash was looped under the handle of a garbage can lid. The lid made a terrible clashing sound as it bounced behind the dog. The dog was spooked by the sound and was trying like the devil to escape the lid as the lid seemed to be chasing the dog. Apparently, our neighbor tied the dog to the lid that was on the can. The dog yanked it, and the lid came loose.

The Bones of the Foot

Major shoe stores in the downtown area had a machine that let you see the bones in your feet. It was free. Standing up, you just stepped onto a platform and inserted your feet into the machine. You could then look down into a small elliptical window. You would see the bones in your feet. They glowed green. I suppose that the machine was for some diagnostic or novelty purpose. It was an x-ray machine. It was a marvel of radiation technology. Did shoe salesmen need to work from X-rays?

Age of Aeronautics

Aunt Ann gave me an old black and white photo of my father from the 1930's. He was wearing a leather aviator's jacket standing next to a propeller driven airplane. The picture was taken out of doors in a field like many of those county airfields that sprang up when aviation was new. Aviation represented the world to come — a new age.

My father spent some of his lunch hours at work building a weather vane for our garage. He made an airplane out of tin. The tin covered a wooden rectangular box. The box had a shaft through its center. The propeller was at the end of the shaft. Bushings were mounted in the rectangular box. The shaft went through the bushings so that a slight breeze would turn the propeller. The plane was mounted on a rod so that the plane could swivel indicating wind direction. As a child, I was impressed by the plane. We had the neatest weather vane in the neighborhood.

As the years wore on, the plane lost parts. Tin fell off of it. The wings broke. My dad removed the airplane leaving the propeller along with the shaft, bushings, and wooden rectangular block that held them. He painted the remains nicely, but it was not the same. Aeronautics was the promise of his youth that vanished leaving a mechanical weather vane. It no longer signified a new age. It no longer expressed optimism.

Big Church, Right Church

After my first communion, I went through a pious phase. I prayed every night. When I was about nine years old or so, I earnestly prayed for things before going to bed. I got down on my knees, put my hands together, and bowed my head. I tried to give the prayers oomph by mouthing them silently as if I were shouting. My face was beet red when I did this. I thought that the intensity was more likely to get God's attention. It would express sincerity. It did pass through my mind, however, that there were millions of people praying for things when I prayed for mine. God was supposed to be in three persons, but even so, the three persons could only take up a few prayers and answer them on any given evening.

One Sunday when entering the church, I became immediately impressed at how big the church was and at how magnificently decorated it was. I thought that the size of the building meant that church teachings were right. They couldn't be wrong with so much wealth and glory behind them. No one would put so much money into a grand building if there were any doubt about church doctrine. The nuns told us that God deserved a big beautiful house.

The nuns said God was present when a certain candle was burning. It was in a chandelier that hung on a wire from the center of the church ceiling. I studied that candle and saw the flame flicker. This told me that God was there. But then I thought, "What happens when the candle burns out? Does God leave until the custodian replaces it?" The nuns also presented bible stories as literally true. The stories seemed to be fantastical. The stories conflicted with my school science courses. I asked my mother whether the Bible stories were true, and she said that the nuns were probably right even though she admitted that some of the stories were hard to believe.

After studying the organs of the human body in public school, I asked my mother, "Where is the soul? Is it next to the heart? The stomach?" My mother said that she didn't know. I told her that the nuns said that the soul was pure white and when we sinned, the soul acquired a black spot. A soul with many sins on it would be speckled, spotted, and dirty looking. I thought that we could check out the soul, as an organ, for spots. This would be a way to show how much sinning a person had done.

The Very Thought of No God

Cleveland had its own political TV commentator named Dorothy Fuldheim. She was a short Jewish lady who always looked very old. She had great credibility with the public. She spoke from the heart and almost always spoke her mind. But it was her no-nonsense attitude that made her convincing. My parents thought that you could believe Dorothy Fuldheim.

One of her opinions, though, we took with a grain of salt. Flying saucers were quite a favorite media topic in the 1950's. In the Cleveland area, a fairly large number of cars developed pits in their windshields. No one could explain it. No kid with a BB gun was shooting holes in car windows. Official Cleveland was baffled. Night after night more pits were reported. Night after night Dorothy Fuldheim mentioned the mystery. Finally, she suggested that the holes were the result of the exhaust from flying saucers! She said it with great conviction.

Fuldheim was a Cleveland institution. She was on TV for probably thirty years. One day she talked about religion. It had something to do with some religious group trying to gain some political advantage. She mentioned the freedom of religion and then said that our society included some people who even were atheists who didn't believe that there was a God. This startled me. I thought that everyone believed in God. It seemed incomprehensible to me that someone could not believe that there was a God. I wondered, "How could they believe that?" It left me emotionally unsettled. It also opened up room in my mind and heart for other possibilities.

Chapter III

Cuban Heels

The junior high years awakened my instinct for fashion. Fashion impressed our friends and helped us make new ones. What were the other kids wearing? The D.A. haircut was in. This was short for duck's ass. It was called that because hair on the sides of the head were greased and combed back to form what looked like the backside of a duck. I think that Elvis had something to do with it. I let my hair grow. I greased it back. I had my D.A. I was ready to fit in with the guys and attract the girls.

Cuba was in the news a lot, and Cuban fashions were a fad and the heels were part of it. I bought a pair of spades; they were the black shoes with tips in the shape of a pointy triangle. Other kids in junior high had Cuban heels so I bought spades with some. They were higher than regular heels, and they were made of wood. You could clog around in them making an impressive racket. The ultimate though was to put horseshoe cleats on the Cuban heels. I got some. The cleat was in the shape of a horseshow that rimed the heel. It was about a quarter of an inch thick. We were taller yet and noisier. Yeah!

To go with the shoes and haircut, you needed pants. I saw a couple of guys wearing toreador pants. They were made out of a silk-like material with what looked like a built-in cummerbund— no belt loops, just snaps, riding quite high on the waist. The snaps had mother-of-pearl centers. Bring on the ladies! There were ruffled shirts, but they didn't attract me. No guys at the school wore ruffled shirts. There was also a gaudy blue shirt with short sleeves. It had silver metallic thread woven into the blue field. Now that was a shirt!

Some of these fashion gems were worn with clothes gotten as presents, usually Christmas presents. Well, they didn't match, didn't coordinate, and looked pretty bad.

Girls typically wore tight skirts above the knee and pressed white blouses that looked very neat. Girls wore circular pins in silver or gold. It was about an eighth of an inch thick with a large hole in the middle. Girls called them virgin pins. They were always a good conversation starter.

Fin Cars

The Russians launched their satellite Sputnik in 1957 and the space race was on. American car manufacturers came out with lines of cars with emphatic aerodynamic looks to them — usually sleek lines and tail fins, you know, like rocket ships. The cars of the late 1950's and early 1960's, were longer than previous cars. In the neighborhood, garages were built in the 1930's and 40's to accommodate shorter cars. People with short garages had a choice. They could leave the garage door open with the tail of the car, fins and all, sticking out. Or they could close the garage door part way, down to the trunk of the car. Or they could add a couple of feet to the front of the garage with the door mounted in it. The addition was usually a protuberance only where the garage door was. You could go up and down the street and see who had a car with fins by checking out which garages had protuberances.

Floating Down the Stairs

On a number of nights, I had the same floating dream. It was such a vivid dream that I could swear I was floating. I was so convinced by the dream that I thought that when I awoke, I could just rise above the ground. The dream was always about going to the top of the stairs. Instead of taking the first step down, I would step into space and gradually descend in the air. It was as if I weighed the same as a feather. I was tempted to try to float down the stairs. I thought that I could do it. I always lost nerve at the top step because I did not feel myself lose my weight. Even so, I still thought that I could do it.

Bum Patches

One Halloween when I was 12 years-old I wanted to dress as a bum. I mentioned to mom that I needed patched pants. She said I would have to make them. She gave me the patch material and the pants. I cut holes in the pants and sewed the patches over them. When she saw what I was doing she said "Oh! No! just sew them onto the pants." When the patched pants were no longer needed, the patches could be removed and the pants used as before. I ruined a good pair of pants. My mother had a good laugh over this.

A Trick Beer

We had family reunions usually in the country. That year we were at Aunt Ann's. The extended family included my father's uncles and cousins. There were over fifty people there. Most of them we did not see during the year between reunions. The men liked beer. They drank lots of beer. A washtub was filled with ice and in it was a couple of cases of beer. Some of my cousins, who I rarely saw, were there. I enjoyed being with them. One cousin, Ernie, was mischievous like me. We came up with the idea of concocting a trick beer. We took an empty beer bottle and filled it with sugar, pepper, Tabasco sauce, anything we could find in the kitchen that seemed horrid. We put a cap on the bottle and buried it in the washtub. We waited for our victim.

We talked about what was about to happen. Someone would taste the bad beer. Spit it out, and say, "Fooey! Who is playing on a trick on me?" Business did not satisfy our eager anticipation. It was not as fast as we thought it would be. We waited and waited. My father came for a beer but did not take the bad one. Other men took beers. Business fell off. Ernie, his brother Richard, and I commented that probably the biggest drunk would get the bad beer. Then along came my father again.

I said to Ernie and Richard, "That's my dad. He's back for another one." He was well along in his beer consumption. His eyes were glassy. He had that smile on his face that said he was in no pain. He took the bottle. We watched his face. He popped the cap, put the bottle to his lips, but smelled the foul odor. He looked surprised, but tried not to show it. He put it down. Didn't say a word. A serious look came over his face. He did not look around to see if he was victim of a prank. He took another beer, opened it, and carried on. Shucks!

Air Raids

It was the early 1950s, and the TV was full of military programs explaining how our forces were aligned in the world against the Soviet communist forces. I enjoyed playing army. There was much gear from army surplus stores: canteens, ammunition belts and boxes, helmets, and so on. Groups of us formed platoons. We encountered the enemy and shot them up. We hit the ground and threw grenades.

One day, Mr. and Mrs. Masek were watching all of this from their front porch. Mr. Masek commented to my parents that when a war breaks out, they will not want to go. He was a veteran from World War One. We did not pay him any mind.

We knew what an exploding nuclear bomb looked like. The test firings were on TV practically every night in some show or another. Atom and then hydrogen bombs were being tested out west in Nevada or on islands in the Pacific Ocean. They exploded the bombs above ground. Each test was reported on TV. There was even an atomic cannon! It shot an atom bomb some thirty or forty miles! The army called the atomic battlefield, "the battlefield of the future." In the newsreel, there were soldiers with gas masks on advancing toward a mushroom cloud from an exploded atom bomb. They were training for the war to come.

In elementary school, we students were drilled for a nuclear bomb attack. There was supposed to be much flying glass so we were marched into a hallway where there were no windows. We then were told to crouch down with our hands folded behind our heads. The strategy was demonstrated on TV. It was "duck and cover." Kids would do it under their school desks or when outside, jump into a ditch. We were supposed to do this until the "all clear" siren.

We were issued dog tags. They were made of stainless steel. On it, our name was printed along with our religious affiliation. A friend said that the tags were supposed to help survivors identify our bodies and give us a proper burial. We concluded that since every kid had a dog tag, somebody expected that there would be a lot of unidentifiable bodies. On a walk home from school, a friend told me that his father was in the war, and once they found a dead soldier, they would put his dog tag between his front teeth and kick his jaw shut. This was to prevent the tag from being lost when the bodies were handled. I guessed that was o.k., but I moved my tongue down the gap between my front teeth to see where my dog tag might end up.

When in junior high school, there was worry that Soviet bombers would fly over the North Pole and hit us with atomic bombs. Our government set up an early warning radar system in Canada and Nike missile sites around major cities to shoot down the bombers. On TV there were tests of Nike missiles that showed what happened when a World War Two era bomber, unmanned of course, was hit by a Nike missile. It was blown to smithereens. This was supposed to be a confidence builder.

Our junior high school had an air raid siren on its roof. It was loud many blocks away. If an attack was under way, we were supposed to take cover. Periodically they tested the siren. I recall being afraid when the siren went off. That sucker was loud. I told myself that it must only be a test. One day after school, the siren went off, and I asked my mother about it. She said that it was only a test. I felt better. It was not long, however, before I realized that she did not have information about a test. She was just telling me this in order to calm my fears.

The sirens were abandoned when the missile era began in the late 1950s. The Nike missiles were of no use against long-range missiles. With intercontinental ballistic missiles, there was not enough time for most people to get the word to "duck and cover." They removed the sirens from the schools.

The nuclear madness came to a head during the Cuban Missile Crisis in 1961. I was a sophomore in high school. I had a study set up in the basement. I recall listening to the sober radio announcer saying that the Russian ships with missiles aboard were nearing the American interceptor ships. They got closer and closer. I became afraid. I thought that I would die soon through a nuclear exchange. I resolved that whatever time I had left I would try to live for the present by getting out and enjoying life. Pleasure deferral for the sake of distant goals was pointless. As the Russian ships turned around, nuclear war was averted. I got a reprieve.

After that day, my friends and I sought parties, sporting events, weddings, whatever came along. I studied enough to do well, develop some of my abilities, and save face. I thought that it did not matter when I died if I lived a quality life at the moment. Living well for the moment was about all I could do.

I felt some relief. But I hated the fact that my government was treating my life as expendable by taking power over it. They could snuff out my life at any moment. They were doing this because they deliberately targeted Soviet cities, and the Soviets did the same. Each public was held hostage to the government of the other side. This arrangement was the same as my government offering me as a hostage in their power games.

Wrestling

One summer professional wrestling became the fad, and we all took it seriously. We held tournaments. We went to matches. We watched it on TV. We knew all about hammerlocks, the sleeper hold, a half nelson, and the dreaded claw. Ray was a friend up the street. He looked like a professional wrestler. He was about five feet nine but he was built like a box. He had a massive chest, massive legs, and large arms. No one we knew looked quite like him. His football coach, reflecting his unique physique, dubbed him "Stump."

The name fit so it stuck. Stump. Well, Ditch, Stump, and I went to a professional wrestling match in the downtown area. The fans were shouting, screaming, and generally carrying on. We went to see a grudge match between Dick Beyer and Fritz von Erlich. The fake blood capsules were popping. There was blood all over the ring.

We sat up in the rafters of Cleveland Arena — a bowl shaped building. We brought a cooler full of food and pop packed in ice. The final match was a tag team event where the bad guys were the Miller brothers. We were shouting and then Stump began throwing ice cubes onto the rink. He winged a cube and it hit big Ed Miller in the head. Miller reacted to the pain and looked up for who threw the cube. He saw only choirboys.

Uncle John

My Uncle John lived with grandma and grandpa for a good part of his adult life. After service in the Coast Guard during World War Two, he settled into a factory job. He did not finish high school. But he educated himself. He was a seeker after truth. He attended lectures of many kinds. He read books about politics, religion, mysticism, and philosophy. He formed a belief system that he shared only in pieces and only sparingly. For many years, he would visit only once a year at Christmas time. He would bring presents, share some wine, and talk to my parents around the kitchen table. My brother and I would sit silently hanging onto his every word.

He had a twinkle in his laughing eyes when he would say, "What I am going to tell you, don't say anything." As he put his forefinger to his lips, he would say, "Shhhhhh! Shhhhh!" He would then laugh. "You don't want to let anyone hear you. They will think you are crazy. Better to stay quiet." And then he would laugh some more. He did this many times in a visit just before he shared his many views. My father thought that Uncle John was a kook. What he believed was not to be taken seriously. To me, Uncle John was like an underground man. He surfaced every Christmas to pass on snippets of privileged information.

As I learned more in school, I thought that Uncle John couldn't be right about a number of things. In later years, I brought up information contrary to his beliefs. He almost always seemed to have a good answer. What did he believe? He believed that religion was about power and money. Apart from religion, there was a metaphysical realm that priests were hardly aware of. If they were aware of it, they didn't want to talk about it. They didn't want us to know the truth.

Toxins in our food and environment corrupt the vibrations of our being. Consequently, we are no longer able to perceive what is around us. For example, other dimensions exist. There are spirits in those dimensions. The very room we are in is full of them. Most of us can't see them. A spiritually pure person can see them.

Spirits exist without eating food. They don't need it. We are at base spiritual beings. We don't need food either. He thought that if he were spiritually pure, he could get along without food, but he did not believe that he was spiritually pure enough. Disease is all a problem of bodily vibrations. Food and drugs cause disease by interfering with our natural vibrations. Medical science is designed to make us sick and keep us sick. This is done in order for doctors to make a lot of money.

Homogenized milk is toxic. The vibration rate of a cow is different than for a human being. By drinking milk, we grow up big and strong like cows but we are spiritually sick. By taking milk from a number of cows and mixing it together, or homogenizing it, we worsen its effect upon us. In that state, it is not even fit for a calf. The calf is tuned to its mother's milk alone.

Germs don't cause disease. Our bodies are full of germs at all times. The reason why the germs take over is that we are already sick. Proliferating germs is an effect of sickness not its cause. Killing germs, then, does not cure disease. A cure would involve restoring the body's health through improving its functioning. This involves improving its spiritual status — rectifying vibration rates by eating right and avoiding toxins.

The Kinetic Christmas Tree

Uncle Butch had bubble lights on his Christmas tree, so the next year we got some too. They added a motion dimension to the tree and were fun to watch. Our tree lacked a respectable ornament for its top. It should be the featured piece. It should be the one that caps the experience of the tree. It should take you to the mountaintop. It should make the viewer satisfied with the experience of the tree as a total effect.

I decided to use some money from my newspaper route to buy one. The usual solution was an angel. Angels had the right symbolism. They top a tree but also appear to float above it. I would have been happy with a memorable angel. No angel appeared in a store — no angel that I could afford anyway. Then I found an exciting tree topper in a local store. It was plastic in the shape of a half sphere. The half sphere was coated with a film that was just like a mirror. It had a chrome look. The sphere was broken into facets of half-inch squares.

Inside the half sphere was a mock candle. The flame was a white Christmas light with a clip on it. On top of the clip was a little spike. On the spike was a wheel with vanes. As the heat rose from the lamp, it turned the vanes. The vanes interrupted the light from hitting the mirror facets. The effect was like that of a ballroom globe — the sort of globe with mirrors embedded in it. Shafts of light were projected all over the room, and like the ballroom globe, they swept the room like searchlights — dozens of them. Wow!

After cranking up the tree topper, I was impressed with the motion of the searchlights in concert with the bubble lights. The tree was beautiful with its static ornaments, but now, it was dynamic! Motion poured out of it. We had a kinetic Christmas tree! How could it be more so? I began to add tinsel. This was the real tinsel. It was metal. It was not the cheap Mylar that looks and feels like plastic. The more tinsel we had, the greater the reflections off of it. I loaded the tree with tinsel.

I noticed that the other Christmas lights were static. This wouldn't do. I bought wink lights. They were lights that shut off and on in a random way one by one. With the lights going on and off, the bubble lights bubbling, the half sphere projecting search lights all over the room, and the tinsel reflecting the whole shebang, our tree was like no other. It moved. It put on a show. Was I proud of that tree!

Collie Terror

The only reason I was able to get a newspaper route was that I helped an older kid with his. You had to know somebody to get a route. Our family had no connections. By helping the older kid, I got noticed by the district manager. He gave me a route in a poorer neighborhood. The housing was older and not as well kept as in my area a few blocks away.

Near the end of the route at the bottom of a hill, there was a two family, two story house perched on a small parcel with a ten foot cement wall that abutted the sidewalk. You walked up a dozen or so cement steps to reach the level where the house began. There were two rental units with the downstairs empty. Upstairs lived a short thin guy with bloodshot bug eyes. He was haggard looking with greasy hair and about thirty-five. He had a short thin wife with bleached blond hair, a lot of makeup, and lipstick that went well beyond her lips. They had no children but they did have a big collie.

The house kind of gave me the willies. It was old, and it smelled musty. It had red granulated asphalt siding; the stuff that looks like roofing shingles. I was told to leave the paper by their kitchen door. This was up the twelve cement steps, up five interior steps to the first floor and then two more flights to reach the landing by their kitchen door. The owner said that the dog was friendly and not to worry. Most days the dog was in the apartment but it barked wildly when it heard me coming up the stairs. Maybe once a week, the dog was sleeping by the kitchen door. Other times it was somewhere in the hall.

I would get to the top of the cement stairs, and all hell would break loose. When the owner was home, he would collar the dog and quiet it down. I would hand him the paper. Other days I would hear the dog. It would charge me. I carried my papers in a canvas bag that I bought from the newspaper company. It had a shoulder strap. As the dog would charge, I would hold the bag in front of me to prevent the dog from getting near my legs. As I made it to the cement steps, the dog would back off.

Sometimes I would be in the house and somewhere on the stairs. I would hear the maniacal bark and the claws of the dog slipping on the stairs as it tried to build a head of steam to come after me. I would flatten against the stair wall trying to figure which direction it was coming from. Needless to say, I dreaded delivering that paper. Mom said that I should refuse to deliver the paper, but I knew that my district manager would frown on that. I tried to figure my way out of the problem.

I decided that a box of dog treats might pacify the dog. As I would hear the dog coming, I would set down a dog treat several feet from me. The dog would lap it up. I would back up a few steps and put down another. I backed up some more and put down another all the way to the cement steps where the dog lost interest.

The treats worked, but I went through a lot of them. I was never sure whether it would continue to work. When the dog heard me, his affect never changed, and he would more quickly lap up the treats so I got fewer steps per treat. That dog didn't want to let me go. I worried that one day I would have no treats and then what? The bug-eyed owner was also slow in paying me for his papers, and he never gave me a tip. Now newspapers are delivered from a moving car by throwing them in the street in front of a house.

A Blizzard of Paper

I lacked impish motivation. I was slow on the uptake. Other kids would act out, you know, kind of explode. I would sit back and maybe get involved late in the game. We had these study halls. There were forty to sixty students in a double classroom. One day our study hall monitor was our social studies teacher Mrs. Whipple. She was near retirement with very white hair, short in stature, easily subject to flattery, and usually not tuned into her surroundings. She always had an armful of books.

In her social studies class, she defended the Bell Curve. She talked about it like it was some rule of nature. Most students were in the center of the bell. The exceptional students were few in number at one extreme and the slow students were at the other extreme. She seemed mystified when she said that it <u>always</u> worked out that way. There just had to be exceptional, average, and below average students in certain proportions. And most students were average. She seemed to think it a marvel that reality could be so organized. Most of us had to be average. So, it came out that way in her class——- mostly C grades.

That was just peachy to her. It was scientific.

The study hall was a few minutes from beginning, and I got there early. Some students arrived shortly after me. They were talking loudly and began to throw spit balls. We called them "spit balls" but they were really just wads of paper. As more students entered the room, they joined into the mayhem throwing with abandon.

Meanwhile, I sat there waiting for the session to begin. I was just watching the blizzard of paper pass me by. It was a blizzard. At any one moment, dozens of pieces of paper were suspended in the air and then rained down. Mrs. Whipple wasn't on time.

There was so much paper, it looked like snow. Wow, this looked like fun. Finally, I thought, "Oh, what the heck." Yowee! I picked up a piece of paper, stood up, and threw it with all my might. Meanwhile, I hadn't noticed that a lookout tipped off the class that Whipple was coming. The class had sat down and all had gone quiet. I was the only one standing! Mrs. Whipple called me up to the front of the room and asked me to pick up all the paper. You couldn't see the floor but for all of the paper on it. I looked like the instigator. My luck.

Summer and Freedom

Summer vacation was breathing space. Someone in our neighborhood would come up with an activity. It would catch on. It would become an obsession. Interest would wear out. We would move on to another activity. We made match guns out of clothes pins. You take a spring clothes pin, remove one side of it, turn the spring upside down, and stick the whole thing into the opening of a regular clothes pin.

You cock the spring, take a kitchen match, put the head against the arm of the spring that is between the prongs of the clothespin, and then pull the coiled part of the spring. If all goes well, the match lights and shoots about four feet. We were going through boxes of kitchen matches shooting the lit matches at each other.

Then we did peashooters. We used peas and navy beans. We shot at birds. We shot at each other. We went through bags and boxes of beans. In not much time, the peas and beans began to sprout. The lawns of the neighborhood were full of sprouting plants. There were also large numbers of sprouts growing up on roofs and out of rain gutters. The neighbors never complained. We never did hit any birds.

As the fourth of July approached, contraband fire- works would be sold piecemeal on the street. Fireworks were illegal in Ohio, but legal in Michigan and many other states. There were always enough entre-preneurs who would make the trip out of state in order to make a quick buck. We all tried to build our arsenals. We liked to keep our cherry bombs, hammer heads, M-80's, firecrackers, roman candles, and so on in boxes. We would get out the box and try to impress our friends. The box always smelled like gunpowder. It smelled real. As the fourth approached, the nightly crackle of fireworks increased up to the grand finale on the fourth.

Then there were the front porch Monopoly tournaments. The games lasted days through various forms of bargaining and cheating. There was also a game that all but disappeared called Easy Money — like Monopoly but involving a board with some hip properties. Poker came much later. Summer was time to breath and live free. This feeling lasted until the fourth of July, and even though two thirds of the sum-mer was yet in front of us, the time after the fourth of July was not the same. It always seemed to vanish ever more quickly with school loom-ing on the horizon.

"It" on Swings

The older kids were playing "It" on swings at the elementary school playground. We played hour after hour to the point of exhaustion. Let us say that a swing set with a steel tube frame has three swings. About three feet from a center line, parallel to the swing seats, you draw two lines with a piece of chalk. The objective is for the person who is "It" to tag you before you can swing to the other chalk mark. The person who is "It" has to go around the poles of the swing set. As he nears a pole, you would swing away. He would run around the other way. You would swing back.

If you step on a line, you are "It." If you are tagged, you are "It." If you drag a foot through the center, you are "It." Getting someone to make a mistake is not easy. The person who is "It" exerts himself to the point of fatigue. Every time he misses a tag, the riders on the swings can taunt him. This makes him all the more angry. The older kids resorted to much swearing. To make swinging easier, little kids would lay on their chests. This would make a lower target, and the swing would be easier to maneuver.

Food Like Grandma Made

Cooking by a grandma was overrated. Some grandmothers were great cooks. Others were average. Others never got good at it. We visited my grandparents on my mother's side almost every Sunday. We would usually wear some of our church clothes. We would remove the tie and loosen the collar. My father usually limply went along. He didn't like going there every Sunday, but he knew that he was not to question the visit. He did not bring up the subject. He was smart.

My grandparents always boasted that they neither smoked nor drank. On Easter or Christmas, grandma took a drink, but only one. My dad liked to drink, drank every day, and drank to excess when he could. My grandparents looked down on him. They criticized him to my mother by always pointing out indirectly that, "We don't smoke or drink. We are smart. We save money." Needless to say, the visit to grandma's was dry. This put my dad in a somber or at least serious mood.

Grandma was not good at entertaining. We sat in the living room in a circle. Little was said. There was no TV or radio. We sort of looked at each other. Grandpa spoke very little English. He could not carry a conversation. Whenever you spoke to him, he would say, "Shoo, Shoo," meaning "Sure, Sure." It never seemed that he got our messages. My dad often made little digs about the lack of conversation such as, "We'll go there and stare at each other." My mother and her mother got on famously. They talked and talked in a mixture of English and Slovak.

As we sat by the dinner table one Sunday, grandma brought in some of her famous rolls. They were heavy, solid, flour and water rolls and quite tasteless. After grandma left the room, my dad said, "Don't drop one on your foot." We cracked up. We also worried about chipping a tooth. Food like grandma made was on the short side of daily fare. As we would slowly work away at the food, Grandma would encourage us by saying, "Eat! Eat!"

The Life Message

I was in the transition to manhood. We were visiting grandma and grandpa. I was sitting at the kitchen table eating a piece of bread and butter. Grandpa walked in. He got a bowl of soup with a big portion of fatty meat. There was a large chunk of fat dangling from the meat. He enjoyed it. He lived a Spartan life — simple food and simple pleasures. As he was eating his soup he said, "Ray, I tell you something. I tell you something."

I was surprised that after all these years, he never said anything to me as a person. He wanted to tell *me* something! His English was minimal. He always showed me things. "Look Ray, cherry," as he pointed to cherries on the cherry tree. I thought that he couldn't say much or that he was not interested in speaking to me. If he wanted to, he could have asked my grandmother to translate for him. But he didn't. I always thought that he didn't want to converse with me or my brother because we were children.

Now, I had passed over to adulthood. He was going to give me some life advice. I never expected any advice from him. But since he brought it up, I eagerly waited for his counsel. Then the moment came; the drum rolled, and he said, "Ray, don't marry Hungarian!" I was taken aback. After twenty-two years of little communication, this is what I have been waiting for? I later gathered that he had a deep hatred of Hungarians because the area of Slovakia from which he emigrated had Hungarian overlords.

Continental Classroom

Mom always protected my sleep. She got me to bed the same time each night. She woke me up the same time each morning. No teacher at school could say that my brother and I came to school half asleep. We were well rested. We were also well fed. Mom always prepared a big breakfast with lots of eggs and bacon. Sometimes I had trouble concentrating in class because I was so full. Later in life, I thanked mom for helping me form regular habits.

When we were in bed, we were supposed to sleep. My brother and I often stayed up a while longer being silly and talking uncontrollably. Dad would come to the bottom of the stairs saying, "Go to sleep already or I am coming up." We would get quiet for a while. Then we would start up again. Dad would come to the steps and say, "Don't make me come up there." The next time he would start up the stairs and then retreat. At this point, we knew he was serious. We went to sleep. In spite of our playing around, we still had at least eight hours of sleep.

The space race was on and television was presented as an educational medium. One program that was supposed to jump-start serious public education was Continental Classroom. College teachers would present college courses to the public. Adults could take the courses for credit. When I heard about the show, Chemistry was offered. What in the world was Chemistry? I was thirteen years old. It sounded interesting. Besides with the Russians beating us in space, we Americans needed to catch up. The only problem was that it was on at six in the morning.

I told mom that I wanted to wake up at six in order to hear a lecture on chemistry. "That is too early. You need your sleep." "Will you set the alarm Mom?" "O.k." The next morning mom didn't wake me; I slept right through Continental Classroom. I then told mom that I wanted to learn chemistry. I told her that I would wake up myself. She didn't have to wake me. The next morning when I went downstairs, there was mom. We watched it together. I don't think that she understood any of it. I understood little of it, but it seemed impressive that the lady professor could know so much and be so good at talking about it.

The next morning, I looked sleepy while watching a presentation on spectroscopy. Mom thought that I was torturing myself. I said, "Aren't the different spectrums of elements neat, the way the bands vary?" Mom didn't think they were so neat. I wanted to send away for the program guide. It was a too expensive. After a few more discussions about valences and ions, I gave up the show. As Mom repeated, "It is on too early. You need your sleep."

What to Live For

The warm sun shone through the living room window in high Spring. I was about thirteen and mulling some "whys" of things. I had heard about some teenager who committed suicide. The shock of it had already run through my emotions. I had felt the gaping hole open up. I asked myself if suicide made sense. For me, it had to come from desperation. Somebody who felt good wouldn't end their life. If you felt good, there would be no urge to end it all.

The religion I had drifted away from taught that we are eternal. This life is the preparation for the life to come. This life is short while eternal life, well you know, is forever. I asked myself, "Why shorten this life to enter life ever after?" You could answer that you can't wait to meet God. That did not occur to me at the time.

It did occur to me that The Church came up with the mortal sin of suicide to keep people from exiting early. Commit that sin and you won't land in heaven but in that other place. So even if this life is unbearable, we are supposed to stick with it. Since God created everything and since pain and suffering exist, it must be part of God's plan. Some think that suffering is for bettering souls to ready them for heaven. It is better to suffer than not.

Well, that's the sort of thing I was thinking about on that sun-filled morning in my living room. I began to consider what rationale we could have for living besides the eternal reward. I thought that in order to give up something important, like my life, I would need to know what I have. Just what would I be giving up? I didn't know. What is life? What was it to me then as a thirteen-year-old? I didn't know. I thought that the best course was to live to find out what life is. If I could answer that question, I could decide whether the rest of it was worth living with all of its experiences good and bad.

If I did not find out what life is, my life would end anyway in a short number of years. This was already very clear to me. I knew my life span was a drop in the cosmic bucket. I had read that the universe was 11 billion years old. So, on that day, I set out to live life to find out what it was about. Little did I realize that aims of life were hard to pin down. Over time I came to the conclusion that many ideas used to make sense of life were vague and subject to long, jumbled discussions.

Take some meaning that kept us going. Some say we should live for today. Suppose today was agonizing. Just what does that mean? Could I legitimately generalize the agonies of one day? If not living for today, I could think I would live for a better tomorrow. But what was that like? Was a better tomorrow likely to happen? Or, I could have changed my aim into hope that my children would have a better life. Better how? If that was off the table, I could have hoped that the world would become a better place tomorrow. But what did that have to do with me? And so on. We could come up with any number of reasons for going on if we had an upbeat attitude about it. Having a clear rationale to live was the issue. It's easy to say but hard to understand.

Looking back on that day, I had the idealized thinking of a young person. As I lived, very predictably, experience reduced that idealism. If we let experience have its way wholesale, we can end up being a cynical old person or even, as Aristotle puts it, someone sour on life. I still can't wrap my head around what life is. As is plain, the questions to be answered keep multiplying. Some of those questions are "why" questions. I have found that "why" questions have few honest answers. We can, however, come to grips with what is <u>important</u> to us in living.

Chapter IV

The Lost City

As we moved into our teens, the guys and I rode our bicycles further from home. Ditch told us about the lost city. I had trouble imagining where it was. South of the neighborhood, there was an industrial area that grew up around The Beltline Railroad. The railroad was built in the 1920's and 1930's. It had a lot of cement infrastructure, arched railroad tunnels, and railroad trestles. The tracks ended up in the industrial valley of the Cuyahoga River — the main artery going through Cleveland. A pocket valley preceded the main one and that was where Ditch found the lost city.

We parked our bikes at the top of the cliff and scrambled to the bottom. We were in a lush valley with ruins here and there. We first came upon a large factory that had a thousand small paned windows most of which were broken. The factory floor was an enormous cement pad. The ceiling was two stories up and part of the roof had fallen in. Beyond the factory we found a fast-moving stream. We waded through it while I worried that it might sweep us away. Up above in front of us was the railroad line. One part of it ran through a cement tunnel. Above it ran another line that joined a high railroad trestle.

As we moved into the valley, there was an old brick kiln with bricks strewn all around. Beyond the kiln was a blue/green pool. It looked like a peacock feather. The water had a coppery color. We thought that the water was polluted so we stayed away from it. Ringing the valley were some waterfalls. They dropped about fifty feet. All of this was an exotic local right in the heart of the industrial city. We excitedly talked about how all that we discovered came to be.

Mind-Rot Science Fiction

We were in bed by ten o'clock. During the summer, my brother and I listened to the radio in bed. We heard a number of shows like The Lone Ranger and The Adventures of Sherlock Holmes. The Holmes show always opened with Holmes playing some abstract violin music. It was lush and rich and painted a warm mood. The show that haunted us, however, was X Minus One. The stories were science fiction. They gave us the willies. Dolls came to life and had bad intentions. Roads roll along from place to place like giant conveyor belts. Aliens were taking over. The shows made me uneasy. My confidence in my security and sense of self were slipping. My grip on reality was getting to be up in the air. I had trouble sleeping. We stopped listening to science fiction.

Delay Firecrackers

Faking people out was a preoccupation of some older kids. There was some joy in this. My friends and I weren't preoccupied with faking people out but we did made our contribution to the effort. The fuses of two-inch firecrackers had gunpowder in them in order to make them burn quickly and uniformly. We would unroll the fuse and remove the gunpowder. The fuse would take up to a minute to explode the firecracker. Without the gunpowder, some fuses went out.

After preparing a number of firecrackers, we would walk the neighborhood lighting and dropping firecrackers. We would be up to a block away before they went off. By then other people, pets, and cars were supposed to be in the vicinity. Boom! They would look to see who threw the firecracker. There was no one in sight. We would get a charge out of startling people. Most of them, however, went off with no one around.

Rodent

Tom lived a block away. We went to public school together from elementary school through part of college. We called him Rodent because he would eat anything. When we visited people, Rodent would sniff out a snack. He had a great sense of humor and was always animated — a natural comic similar to Jerry Lewis. Many of our families had grandmothers living in, and they liked to cook. The food was especially good during the holidays. Whatever food grandmothers offered Rodent he ate. Whatever food anyone offered Rodent, he ate. But he got the name when he took a piece of chocolate cake, put it in a bowl, poured milk into the bowl drowning the poor cake — causing it to disintegrate. It looked gross. White soup with chocolate floaters. Because of this act, Ditch thought Tom earned the nickname.

Hanging Out on the Rock

We spent much time hanging-out on "the rock". It was a sixty foot stretch of 2' by 2' cut stone set on the lawn edge of the elementary school right next to the sidewalk. We would sit on the rock, talk, and fool around. The rock faced an intersection with the two- lane main street intersected by a side street. There were three stop signs. The intersection was in the heart of the neighborhood with a constant flow of cars usually arriving one at a time. The flow was constant because it was the principal way to go around the elementary school. There was a popular deli and beverage store across the street from it.

We got in the habit of waving to the drivers of cars and I think this came about by accident. One of us waved at someone he thought he knew, the person waved back, and then we realized that we didn't know him. Well, Stump got the idea that if you catch someone with a wave as he is pulling away from the stop sign, he does not have time to see whether he knows you, but he will wave back and then look to see who you are. Of course, he realizes at that moment that he does not know you, and often that he has been had. So, for fun, we would sit on the rock and time our waves and stranger after stranger would wave back.

Once Ditch's cousin was visiting him, and he sat on the rock with us. We waved at everyone, most of them waved back, and he commented that, "You guys know everyone, don't you?" We then let him in on our trick.

My Girlfriend is Pregnant Again

Ditch, Stump, and I took a bus to downtown Cleveland. We would set out to buy some minor clothing item, but the real reason for the trip was a little adventure and to pass time. There were two big department stores on Public Square. Each had a number of floors with escalators running between floors. The up and down escalators on a floor were built right next to each other. If you were going up one of them, you would cross by the other one going down. Imagine an X pattern with each line being an escalator.

As you approached the people going the other way, they could pick up some of your conversation and you could pick up some of theirs. We launched into mock conversations that people going the other way would hear. Stump would say, "My girlfriend is pregnant again." Ditch would say, "For the third time?" Stump would say, "I don't know what our parents are going to do." We would plan it so that the other people could hear the gist of the exchange.

You should have seen the disapproving looks on some of the people. We were all of fourteen! Of course, we thought that this was a lark. The aim was to get a rise out of people. I think that we set the youth of the city back years in the eyes of some of the public.

Drag the Bag

On hot August nights, people would sprinkle their lawns just before dusk. The lawns were not large. The usual way to do it was to stand on the sidewalk; from there you could reach the tree lawn and the front lawn without stepping on the grass. The men were usually in their under shirts. Other people would sit on their front porches, talk to each other and to passersby. After dark the mosquitoes would get bad and people would go inside for the evening.

I don't know who invented Drag the Bag. I don't know if it was a national trend or whether some diabolical local teenager had thought it up. One of my brother's friends told us about it, and so we tried it. You take a thirty-foot length of string and tie it to a small brown paper bag. The bag should be about the size that you would be given when buying candy. The bag should be left open with the string tied to one corner of the opening. You then tie the string to your leg just above your ankle.

Starting at the corner of a street, you set the bag down and let the string play out. When it is getting dark, people on the front porches can't see the string. People watering their lawns won't notice the string. The bag makes the darndest motions and rustling sounds. When you take a step, the string brings the bag along one step. You would swear that the bag was some kind of animal. It seemed for a brief second to be alive. When you would step with the other foot, the bag would rest. With the next step, it would scurry another two feet.

To get the full hilarious effect, you need a confederate — someone who is watching the expressions of the people as they encounter the bag. You will never forget their fear and surprise that turns to anger or disgust. One night I was following a bag dragger, and as the moving bag came into view and made the rustling sound, two people on porches bolted to a standing position holding onto the railing. They peered at it. What was it? A bag? Then they became deflated when realizing that it was a prank. Another guy was watering his lawn when the bag scurried by his legs. He jumped out of the way, thinking that it was a sizable animal. Whoa! Better safe than sorry!

Bison

According to Bill, his father was always getting on his case. They lived in different universes. Bill was academic; he was a reader. Bill followed the lead of his mother who was a librarian. His father wasn't academic. Bill said that he was defensive about himself and disapproving of Bill. He often put Bill down, and Bill was very emotional about it. I think that his father didn't know what space to give Bill without compromising his position. So, they were perpetually dancing around each other.

We became high school buddies, and as Bill met the other guys — Ditch, Rodent, and Stump — we decided that he needed a nickname. Rodent was the one who insisted on calling me "Boose." It was short for caboose — the last car on the train. He said it fit me because I always came in first. It's sort of like calling the tall kid "shorty." In reality, I did not come in first. I was a middle of the pack kind of guy or maybe a little beyond middle. The mass society taught me well. There was always someone better than you in any given area. It's supposed to promote anonymity. It's supposed to make you accept your fate, you know, "settle for" what comes. Why? Well, that's another story that I won't start on now.

We tried a number of names for Bill until Rodent came up with "Bison." Bill was happy with it. He was now one of the guys. Rodent explained in utter seriousness that Bison was like a bull in a china shop. By the time Bison would be done, something would be broken. He had a talent for making the awkward comment. For instance, when we were putting someone on, and the person acknowledged that they knew they were being put on, Bison would wreck the moment by blurting out the truth saying that we were putting the person on. He did this to deliberately undermine the humor in the situation or so I thought. The rest of us just said, "Shut up Bill; don't spoil it." But we liked Bison. He had no pretenses even though he was smarter and knew more than we did.

One Glove Experiment

The worst part of the walk to high school was the trek across the open asphalt expanse by the elementary school. In frigid winter, the wind hit you head on. And then you crossed near the corner of the building and a blast of cold air whipped you. It was only about five minutes of the walk, but I came to dread it. One day I realized that I had only one glove. I had lost the other. I decided to put on the left glove so that at least one hand was warm.

I noticed that the bare hand was not as cold as it should be with no glove. I did not end up with one hand with numb fingers and the other hand acceptably warm. The next day and the day after, I deliberately wore one glove. I concentrated on the bare hand as being like the gloved hand. It seemed to work. I thought that we were creatures with parallel sides. The body would treat the warmth of one hand as the norm for the other. This seemed to be encouraged by concentrating on one hand being warm.

Doorless Vintage Cars

Rick's father always bought an old car, a beater, for transportation to work. He was a rather good judge of cars; he knew just about how much life they had left in them. Rick was not quite sixteen and wanting a car of his own, and he begged and begged his father for the 1953 Chevy. His father endlessly refused. Rick said that his father intended to use the car for ice fishing on Lake Erie.

Rick's dad was an avid fisherman. When the schools of fish were running in Lake Erie, he would come back with over one hundred white bass or yellow perch. He and Rick would clean and freeze them. In the winter, the Lake froze over, and near the islands on Lake Erie, many fishermen would set up their ice-fishing shacks and pull in quite a few fish. The way to get to the islands was by car, across the ice. The ice was uneven in places and there was always the danger that the ice would crack and the car plunge to the bottom.

For safety sake, the drivers would remove the doors from the cars. If the ice started cracking, they would bail out before the car went under. Needless to say, with no doors the drive to the islands was very cold. Over the years, many cars were lost. They sit at the bottom of Lake Erie. They are vintage old cars without doors.

A Real Double Date

Rodent's mother was going to throw a hemorrhage, at least that was the way that Rodent put it. This was his first date. His mother worried whenever Rodent got near a girl. She became hysterical warning Rodent that some girl would try to trap him by getting pregnant. We were all of fifteen. At that time, most kids of our age were very far away from having intercourse. Rodent and I never thought that any girl would "go all the way." I think if any girl led us in that direction, we would have put on the brakes.

Rodent asked Mary Ellen to the dance, and she accepted. The date was on. After school I visited Rodent to plot his escape. After he told his mother about the date, she threw a fit. Whenever girls were concerned, his mother saw no good. She would launch into the "you whoremaster!" speech. It was blood curdling. We retreated to Rodent's basement. He snuck his suit into the basement. His plan was that after dinner he would go to the basement, change clothes, and make a break for the side door. That was risky, so we tried to find another way.

His house had a front porch enclosed with lattice. In the basement, there was a wooden insert the size of a basement window facing the porch. It seems there was a window there before the front porch was added. We took screwdrivers and pried the caulk from the wooden door figuring that he could sneak out under the front porch. We worked at getting the insert loose. Dirt was falling on the floor. It took both of us to hold the thing in place, trying to prevent it from falling. Then its weight caused it to slip and a burst of snowflakes blew in. We turned our heads sideways as the blast of snow hit our faces. There was Rodent's mom standing right behind us! After another round of the "You whoremaster" speech, Rodent learned that he was not only confined for the night but that his mother would keep vigil.

There was a pretty girl in homeroom, and I asked her to the dance. Rodent and I planned to double date. Her name was Ermaine Lade. She was more mature than I was; she already had some dates with Chucky Rossiter who was sixteen and had a car. Ermaine was infatuated with Chucky. I didn't have a car. Rodent and I were going to walk to our dates' houses and then take two buses to get to the sock hop. Ermaine said she didn't mind, but she did date Chucky Rossiter who did have a car. She was in awe of Rossiter but he had other girlfriends. A kid in our homeroom named Jim went around homeroom saying that Ermaine's middle name was "was." Then to make it obvious, he would say with deep sincerity, "Ermaine "was" Laid," get it?" "We got it Jim. We got it." Ermaine didn't take his bait. She was quiet and dignified.

Mary Ellen and Ermaine were friends. The double date was on. Then disaster struck. Rodent went to the basement and changed into his suit. He made a dash for the side door, but he had trouble unlocking it. His mother nailed him. She grabbed him by the collar. He was in for the night.

A flurry of phone calls led to me taking both girls to the dance. Did my two dates make me cool? You guessed it. The two girls had a merry time talking up a storm. I was more the tag along. We were standing on a street corner waiting for the crosstown bus. They started to giggle. I said what's up? They continued to giggle and pointed across the street. I looked. I still didn't get it. Then I realized a store sign said "Hardware" Store. Finally, I got it. Hard wear. You got it? Oh well!

The dance was at Saint Michael's hall. They played 45rpm records. There were some crepe paper streamers and a few colored lights. We danced a bit. I made sure that Tom's date did not feel like a third wheel. Here I was with two dates! My first date and it was with two girls! I continued to see Ermaine but I got tired of hearing about Chucky Rossiter. We decided to be friends.

The Tokens "Tina"

Round about tenth grade, we would treat ourselves to pizza. At that time, pizza was not a staple but an Italian specialty. The neighborhood parlor was Pepe's. It was several blocks away. On Friday night with little to do, we walked to Pepe's. They had the good old Wurlitzer jukebox. People took turns feeding it quarters. We often did not play it because we didn't have extra money. When we did play it, we wanted to make a statement about our extra cool taste in music.

Ditch, Rodent, Stump, Rick, and I all liked the Tokens' "The Lion Sleeps Tonight." When we had spare change, we played it. Then Rick played the flip side — a song called "Tina." It was kind of droll and repetitious, and part of it seemed to be in Hawaiian or something. Phonetically it went, "Tina, sangu, lay law by ty you, watch out, watch out, watch out. Watch out. Watch out. Watch out, watch out, watch out. Hey Ti—ee—na." And then the whole verse would repeat again and again. The Tokens infused pep into the delivery even though the melody was quite a monotone. During the song, Stump looked at Rick in an approving way. We all thought that it was pretty good.

We did kind of notice that its repetitiousness made it somewhat wearing. The droll vocal line made it kind of obnoxious. We all bounced along to it. Then Ditch decided to play it again. And again. Pretty soon we were looking for a response from people sitting around us. They didn't seem to care. I suppose that they came for the pizza. Every time we played the song, we couldn't help but laugh. We bounced along to it. Whenever we went to Pepe's, and we had some extra money, we would serenade everyone with a few encores of Tina.

Caroling

Rick decided to go around Christmas caroling in order to raise money for the holidays. He was taking accordion lessons at the time. The accordion was bigger than his chest. I did not envy him lugging that thing around. He was pretty good at playing it. He knew a number of carols, but he did make some mistakes. Neither of us was a very good singer. I had trouble staying in tune. We were not the most talented carolers. But it was the spirit of the thing that counted? Right?

We went porch to porch. Some people were very nice. They listened to a carol and then gave us some money. We noticed after a while, though, that some people gave us the money without our doing very much. We suspected that they just wanted us to leave their porch. They were probably not impressed with our performance. Of course, they were smiling all the while. They tried to stay in the spirit of the season.

Other people refused to answer the door. In response, we sang louder and with less of the Christmas spirit. If we thought that we were being snubbed, we gave a few loud encores before we left. We did this especially when someone seemed to be hiding out in there, trying not to be seen.

Carrying a Conversation

I had trouble phoning girls to ask them on a date. Most of the girls in school were casual acquaintances. Most hadn't dated. Most hadn't had a boyfriend or any guys interested in getting to know them. I would look up their numbers in the phone book. It took some courage to make the call. My palms would sweat. My voice would be weak. I would usually get their father or mother. I could detect surprise on the other end of the line by the parents. They were polite, but I could tell that most had not adjusted to boys calling the house.

If the call went badly. Or if I sounded awkward. Or if I said something private, I didn't want my parents to hear it. Like most everyone else, we had one phone. It was on the landing of the stairs. When someone was on the phone you could hear every word throughout the house. Our house was small. Also, our phone had, what was called, a party line. Another family in the neighborhood shared the same line. Sometimes when you picked up the receiver, you would hear them on the line. You would come back in a few minutes to hear if they were still on the line. They had to hang up before you could make your call. Likewise, at times they came on the line when you were talking to someone. If they were nosy, they could listen to your every word so long as they were very quiet. But sometimes you sensed that someone was listening.

So, I tried to avoid making calls from home. I walked up to Vatava's Drug Store. It had phone booths. The line in the phone booth was a private line. Sometimes the two booths were occupied. Sometimes you had to wait quite a while to get an open phone. All the while I waited, my nerves would frazzle, and my throat would get so dry that it was hard to talk. I tried to put on a good attitude. "Even if I am rejected, nothing ventured, nothing gained." If I was interested in someone, the least I could do was try.

I worried about running out of things to say. I feared pauses and dreadful silences on the other end. They seemed like forever. I began to prepare for a call. I would jot down a number of topics on a note pad. When a big silence came, I would hit my list and bring something up. I usually got good results. Most girls appreciated my interest even if they had none for me. I was successful most of the time. With some girls, the day after a call, their friends would be abuzz at school when I was around. I could tell that when I hung up, Ma Bell had lit up like a Christmas Tree.

Sometimes a girl sounded tentative. It was always difficult to tell whether she was shy, or not a good conversationalist, or whether she was resisting the idea of me. If she was resisting but agreed to a date, she would be going only to have some fun. The focus was not on me but on the movie or party that we were attending. Other times, a conversation would mushroom easily. Both of us would be happy and laughing and carrying on famously. This was called "hitting it off." Some girls were easily approachable even though they were not interested in me in a romantic way. They were the sort of people that were fun to be around.

I saw Linda at a party and got her phone number from a friend. She seemed kind of deadpan at the party and spoke in a slow way, but she was pretty. I wanted to follow up our encounter. I went to Vatava's and called her.

"Hello, Linda, this is Ray."

"Hiiii."

"I met you at the Alice's party."

"Uh, huuuuh."

"I thought I would give you a call to see how you are."

"Fiiiine."

"Did you like the party?"

"Yeeees."

"How did Alice invite you?"

"I dooon't knooow."

"Do you like school?"

"Nooo."

"Why don't you like school?"

"I dooon't knooow."

"Are your parents home?"

"Yeees."

"Do you have a lot of homework tonight?"

"Nooo."

"What classes do you like?"

"I dooon't knooow."

"Do you like American Bandstand?"

"Yeees."

It went on this way a while longer. It was like pulling teeth. Linda was no conversationalist.

What was peculiar about Linda's answers was that she gave them in a slow soft way. "Yesss." "Nooooo." "I doon't knoow." Ditch talked to her on another occasion and got the same reaction. We laughed about it. What do you do when the only responses are, "Yes," "No," and "I don't know?" I cut through the list of topics that I brought with me to the phone booth. Only a minute had passed and the big long silences were looming. Ten topics gone in a flash with a "Yes," "No," or "I don't know." "Well, errr, nice talking to you. I have to go." And then she said, "Oh!" Her surprise that the conversation was about to end was a surprise to me.

Silent Parties

Our parents agreed to let us have parties in our basements. Rick had a basement that was well painted, clean, and neat. A few decorations later and it was an acceptable party space, that is, to a sixteen-year-old. More than three couples and the party was on. The girls wore party dresses. Their parents dropped them off. We had fruit punch with no "enhancer." Rather than a "punch" we called it a "tap." We played lps — long playing records. Rick's parents enjoyed meeting the girls. The girls were nice and friendly and wholesome. The guys were polite.

The party started with some rock and roll. We danced, ate potato chips, and talked, laughed, you know, we made party sounds. After about an hour, the slow music went on, and we danced. There was no talk. The lights were dimmed. The music stopped. No one went to start another record. The party fell silent. Couples dancing reverted to the dance called "the no step." Stand in one spot and squeeze. The necking and petting were well under way. Rick's parents quickly caught on. "Rick, what are you doing down there? Put on some music, and turn on the lights." The lights went on, and we put another record on. Conversation started up. Fifteen minutes later, the lights were dimmed and the conversation stopped. From the top of the stairs, "Turn on the lights. Is the party over?" We put on a record, but shortly, it became silent again. "If you don't turn on the lights, I am going to make everyone go home."

Chapter V

Being Grabbed

Rodent and I walked together to high school some of the time. I would pass his house to collect him. He was never ready. I would keep saying, "Come on Tom, we have to go." He would be racing around in a state of half dress while trying to gather up his stuff. His mother would be yelling at him to hurry up while reminding him not to forget this or that. He set a record for never leaving on time.

In the winter, it was a cold half-mile walk to the high school. It was a particularly bitter winter, below freezing for weeks on end. The sidewalks were icy. I would walk carefully looking where I was going. Rodent would be distracted, talking away, not looking where he was going. He wore shoes with leather soles. He would slip and slip again. Rather than regain his balance by himself, he would grab onto my clothes to stay up. O.K. if he did it once or twice. No, again and again he was distracted, grabbing onto me, and I am saying, "Let go, what are you doing? Get your hands off of me." "I am slipping, I need to hold on to you." "Why am I not slipping?" "You have better shoes." "I am watching where I am going." And this sort of exchange continued on and on until we reached school.

Academic Opportunity

Jean's parents pulled strings to have her opt out of going to my high school. Her parents got her into the all-white school one district over. At the time our high school was the only integrated high school in Cleveland. This means that some schools were almost all white. Others were almost all black. My school was about half and half. Jean said that her parents did not want her going to school with black kids.

I ran into Jean when we were seniors, and she described her studies. She had little math, little science, and no foreign language. I was surprised. Jean was just about the brightest student in elementary school. In high school, she was far behind kids at my high school including yours truly. It appeared that many of the most talented teachers in the district preferred to teach at the integrated school. The quality of their product was reflected in our school being competitive with some of the best suburban high schools.

Chemistry Class and the Paddy Wagon

Our high school had three thousand students. As an inner-city school, only thirty percent or so took classes like chemistry. The classroom was on the third floor of the building. From its windows you could see the walk up to the front door of the school. In chemistry lab, some of us would sit on the windowsills and look out at the street. Every morning we would see the paddy wagon pull up. Police would enter the building and out they would come with a student in handcuffs. At the time truancy laws were enforced. We could not imagine, though, that truants would be handcuffed. Besides, those taken away were in school at least on that day.

Playing Bass Drum

Veteran marching band members worked into the best positions. I could play snare drum well enough to play with the best snare drummers. As the new kid in the drum section, though, I was given bass drum. It was o.k. On the one hand, it became heavy when carrying it for long stretches of practice. On the other hand, it was easy to march while playing it. The drum set the cadence of the steps. The drum itself was not a very good one. It tended to "boing" rather than "thud." No bass drum should "boing."

Barbara was also new in the drum section. She played cymbals. When we marched in single file, she was in front of me. She had a sense of humor. I also think that she liked me. When we walked out of the stands single file, she grabbed and pulled my bass drum laughing hysterically all the while. I nearly fell over. I told her to stop. I shouted for her to stop. She kept on laughing. She kept on pulling. Then she stopped. We walked a few more steps, and she grabbed it and almost pulled me over. I tried to thwack her with my mallet. I could not quite reach her in front of the drum. This made her laugh all the harder. Fortunately, she stopped doing it when we entered the field to play. I was relieved that I could at least maintain some dignity.

Snow Plow Basketball

One Christmas, Rick's father bought him a snowplow. You stood behind it, and the gas engine would propel it along. It had chains on its tires. This was not the sort of present that Rick wanted, but he smiled and said that the "old man" had plans for him plowing sidewalks for money. His father's idea was give the man a snowplow, and he will earn much money plowing snow. Rick wasn't interested in plowing snow especially during Christmas vacation! You shouldn't have to work during Christmas vacation. Besides, what kind of Christmas present is a snowplow? It is like giving a kid a shovel.

Several of us started a neighborhood basketball team, and over the break, we intended to practice. There was no gym in the neighborhood that we could easily use. The closest basketball court was behind the elementary school, and it was covered with snow. We had a flash of brilliance. Put the plow to use. The snow was deep. It took Rick the better part of an hour to clear the court. He parked the plow, and we played basketball.

Around about three o'clock, his father was driving home from work past the elementary school. He saw the parked plow, the cleared court, and his enterprising son playing basketball. He was steamed. After a hard day's work at his factory job, his son used the plow to hang out with the guys. No money made there. He stopped the car and shouted for Rick to go home. The next day, Rick did not want to talk about what his father did when he got home. He was still not inspired to plow sidewalks.

Prime Parking

High school football games were played at night at the field in the middle of the neighborhood. Across the street from the field, on three of its sides, were rows of houses. Some of the guys in that neighborhood would wait until shortly before the game, when it was already dark, pick out dark houses, and hold up a $1 parking sign. They would stand in the street and flag cars down, parking them all across the front lawns, about four cars per house. After collecting money for the last car, they would be gone in a flash! The people returning home had the initial impression that football fans just decided to park their cars all over their lawns.

Door Prize

We decided to have a party. We wanted to be cool. In those days a mark of being cool was having a good sense of humor. Jokes made for happy talk, and they covered some of awkwardness of being a teen. So, if you were going to have a door prize, what should it be? It came to me in a flash of brilliance — a door. We found a wooden door in Ditch's garage. One of the girls won it. Of course, she didn't want it. None of the girls was impressed. None of them laughed. None of them thought that we were cool.

The Hair Pie

Ditch's cousin lived next door to a family that had only girls — three of them. All were blond and looked like they could be in Breck shampoo commercials. They were cute. The youngest one was attracted to Ditch. He loathed her. He kept making up reasons why he would have nothing to do with her. To keep his blood up, I would innocently say that she was not that bad — the blond hair, blue eyes, cute face. This made Ditch all the more angry.

One day Ditch got roped into attending a birthday party for her at his house. I think that his mother was trying to please his aunt that had something to do with showing hospitality to her neighbors. Ditch came up with the idea of a hair pie. He was sort of obsessed with it. The hair pie. The hair pie. Finally, I said that maybe we should give her as a present, an actual hair pie. Ditch said, "Hey, let's do it." The pie part was easy. We got a pie shell and filled it with whipped cream. The hair part was trickier. None of us had that much hair to spare.

We went to Stutz's Barber Shop. The shop was full of people getting haircuts or waiting to get haircuts. Ditch asked Stutz, "Do you mind if we take some of the hair off of your floor? We need it for something we are making." He agreed. We swept up a nice mound of hair, and we were in business. We wrapped the pie in a nice box with a nice ribbon. The pie itself looked god awful. Greasy hair mounded on whipped cream. Barf!

When she opened the present, she didn't know what it was. None of her girlfriends knew what it was. Ditch said, "It's a hair pie!" They giggled a little, and then said that they thought it was a good joke. I was holding my breath. I thought that her response might get weird. Ditch thought that he might get more of a rise out of her. He wanted her to be mad. That girl just did not want to cooperate. He had to make up more reasons why he didn't like her.

Crashing Weddings

We came upon wedding crashing rather innocently. A friend Nick was going to a wedding and asked if we wanted to come along. We made note of the good company, free food, free drinks for under-aged guys, live music, and lots of new women to meet. After sticking around for an hour, we said bye to Nick and went on with our Saturday night.

In the neighborhood, there were a number of halls that were rented for weddings. Each Catholic church had a hall, and there were private ones as well. Ditch, Rodent, and I hatched the first plot. We bought a wedding card. We put, "To the Bride and Groom," on the envelope. Inside, we put a message like, "Best wishes for a long and fulfilling life together." We signed the card with a fictitious name like, "The O'Malleys." Of course, we put no money in the card. We dressed up in our suits and began scouting the halls for wedding receptions. We needed a large wedding. This would typically have 300 plus people. Bingo! St. Michaels had a reception.

We parked in the church lot and waited for a middle-aged couple with no children to begin walking toward the door. We got in front of them. To a stranger, we appeared to be a family. The stranger we were interested in deceiving was the cop at the door. The church that rented out the hall required a cop at the door. This was of course to guard against undesirables from disturbing the reception as well as keeping order as the guests drank to excess. The cop at the door paid us no mind. We dropped our card in the box for cards. We were in!

The next aim, we agreed, was to fit in. We went to get drinks. We immediately struck up a conversation with someone. This made it appear that he knew us. We asked, "Whose side are you on?" He said, "I'm on Phil's." The next person we met, we asked the same question with the answer, "I'm on Marge's." Everyone we would meet from then on would reveal their side, and we would claim to be on the other. Of course, we would talk about the great day, the beauty of the bride, their suitability as a couple, and so on.

We made some effort to dance with the best- looking girls our age and tried to get phone numbers. But the crowning glory was to participate in the bridal dance. The bride would dance with anyone who put a dollar in a hat. Each dancer had about a minute with the bride. I did the bridal dance and highly praised her looks and gave well wishes. The irony was that at that time, weddings were shot in super-eight film. An eight- millimeter camera mounted on a light bar of blinding lights was used. It required a cord plugged into the wall. Shooting wedding movies was always disruptive. Ditch, Rodent, and I imagined the couple watching the movie asking, "Who are those guys?" They probably tried to tie us to some family or another.

We crashed two or three weddings and then ran into the problem of the same cop working the hall week after week. Now it was possible that we would be invited to weddings week after week because the people getting married were mostly from the immediate community. But when we saw the same cop twice before, we chickened out. We went to other halls. The weddings were too small or we thought that we just did not fit in. This ended my wedding crashing. Ditch and Rodent went on to further adventures, but gave up the practice when Rodent got drunk and sick and ended up with an acute appendicitis.

Kicked Out of the Roxy

There was one burlesque theater left in downtown Cleveland — the Roxy. It was long past its heyday. The shows were just strip shows — no comedians or musical talent. The theater was dirty. The wall fabric was faded. Some seats were torn. The place smelled of decaying plaster. At eighteen Ditch, Rodent, Bison, and I could be admitted, so we headed for the Roxy. That day Rodent was particularly frisky. As the rest of us walked in a group, Rodent ran up one side of the street and down the other. He opened and jumped in a salt box used for salting icy streets.

As the first act began, a rather good looking thirty- fiveish red head came out. The live drummer highlighted her bumps and grinds. Bison began shouting out, "Take it off! You can show more than that!" "You've got a few extra pounds!" "Look at that belly!" We elbowed Bison to shut up. This only encouraged him. He kept after her so that she hardly had time to breathe. The bouncer and cop walked briskly down the aisle and told Bison that he had to leave. He protested as he was escorted to the lobby of the theater.

The Roxy had largely a low-life clientele. The audience was sparse. Most people looked bedraggled except for the occasional guy and his date. We all wondered, "Who would take a date to this show?" At the end of an act a girl would be down to her G-string. Some guy would shout out, "Show us a little." She usually lifted the G-string to give a peek. The blue and red lights and the dim theater assured that the peek was all shadow. The strippers knew there was a limit to how far they could go. There was always a cop at the door who also watched out that no indecency laws were broken.

As the show ended Bison was in the lobby and filled us in about what happened to him. What do you have to do to get kicked out of the Roxy? We were sure that Bison was in elite company. How quickly it happened might even have been a record. Chalk one up for the Bison.

Chapter VI

My Son is at Work

During a hot summer and being drawn to make a show for the girls, the guys and I were interested in throwing a party to end all parties. Our big effort was inspired by Ditch. He suggested that we have a luau. His father's business partner was a chef at one time and agreed to make Hawaiian spare ribs for us. We then began brainstorming the party. Rodent was insistent that we have a tiki for the right event setting. He and Ditch insisted that it be big.

Rick did a drawing of the tiki used in the introduction to the TV show Hawaiian Eye. The drawing was quite good. Now all that we needed was a large tree trunk. Rick's uncle had an old Chevy pickup truck circa 1930's. We took whatever axes were available and set out to find a tree. A dozen or so miles away, we saw a tree that had been blown down in a storm. It was next to the road and appeared to be on a small parcel of vacant land. We set to work. Five of us chopped and chopped. We were exhausted when we finally cut through the tree. The trunk was about six feet high with a diameter of about three feet. We had a whale of a time moving it to the truck and getting it in.

Then the big argument began. Where should we take it? We all knew that our parents would not be happy with it in the yard and all the carving that was about to be done. Finally, Rodent agreed that the work would be done at his house. We plopped it down in front of his garage. Rick traced the image of the tiki on the trunk and we started carving. Rodent's father arrived home after work to the sight of his son working, sweating to make something. It also appeared that his son was the leader of the project. His father was beaming.

Rodent's father apparently wanted his son to find a summer job. Rodent was not inspired. He was not motivated. Or so I thought. Meanwhile his father worked long hard days building doors in a factory. No matter what Rodent did, his father kept talking about his son finding a job. He would get worked up about Rodent's attitude and kept saying that his getting worked up was going to cause him to have a heart attack. Rodent was not moved. So, when his father saw him in an enterprising activity that involved labor, he was smiling ear to ear.

His buoyant attitude did not last long when he asked about the job. He realized that we were not going to make any money. We were going to have a party. His yard was full of wood chips. There was noise and loud music on the radio. His father began to make unpleasant sounds. Why was it in his yard? How did Tom get to be the leader? "You can't have the party in this yard." We negotiated that we be given two more days to finish the tiki and then we would get the thing out of there.

The Luau

Ditch's parents agreed to have the party at their house. Our decorations had some nice flourishes — Chinese lanterns with Christmas lights in them, hollowed out coconut shells for cups, and two torches to flank the tiki. We used old doors on concrete blocks for a ground level table, of course, covered with a tablecloth. Ditch and Rodent set the tiki afire to give it a charcoal patina. It looked great.

Rodent insisted that we have a fountain. He had the idea to arrange three birdbaths so that the top one poured into the second and the second into the third. The only problem was that we had no birdbaths. Rodent and Ditch went on an early morning raid, running through yards absconding with neighbors' birdbaths.

We needed flowers — lots of them. We wanted each person to have a lei. Flowers were expensive. We thought about going around the neighborhood picking what flowers were available. It wouldn't work. A lei required too many flowers. Then I had a stroke of genius. Where were there abundant flowers? In the cemetery! Rodent and Ditch got a friend to drive them to the cemetery. Ditch said that they did not need to take flowers from graves. Used flowers were put in a heap before disposal. We had probably a thousand dollars-worth of flowers. We made the leis.

As the big day approached, the neighbors on the street saw all of the stuff going into Ditch's yard. They knew something major was about to happen. Many stopped by to talk to us and Ditch's parents. There were about ten couples. Our dates were happy to come to the luau. The scene was right out of Elvis Presley's <u>Blue Hawaii</u>. The night, the lights, the Hawaiian music, the great food, the burning torches, the sound of the fountain, the flowers. Then it started to rain. Rodent stood up, and shook his fist at the sky, and said, "You motherless!"

The Tiki Problem

Ditch had the Tiki in his yard. His parents did not want it. Rick could not get his uncle's truck to move it somewhere. Besides we did not want to throw it away. It came out rather well. I came up with a plan. My cousin Beverly married Russ, a reporter for a major Cleveland newspaper. I called Russ and he agreed to write a short article about the problem of the Tiki. We sold the Tiki to a guy who had a lake cottage in Pennsylvania. It may still be there today.

Cheater Trig Pencil

Guys in middle school had a different shop class each term. One of them was print shop. We had a great teacher— Mr. Ribich. He was as manly a man as you could find— a tough world war two veteran with facial scars to prove it. He was a caring teacher to his eighth graders. He told us that if we read about a subject just a half hour a night, by the time we graduated from high school, we would know more about that field than most specialists in it. I think he had a point.

The introductory classes were about safety. He warned us about the paper shear. No one was to lose fingers this term. Rumor had it that in a prior term a student had cut off his hand. He panicked and put it into his back pocket and ran out of the building. Someone had to chase him down and tackle him. It was fortunate that he didn't bleed out.

One of our projects was to learn the type case and do type setting. An individual piece of type was a lead shaft with a print symbol on its tip. It was about the size of a wooden match. These were gathered up from a wooden tray called a type case. Each letter, punctuation mark, and so on had its own little section in the tray. A typesetter would have the boxes memorized so that he could quickly grab pieces of type to form words and ultimately text. A major task in print shop was to memorize the type case.

Some of the guys wanted the lead type. When windows were open in the spring and fall, they would throw pieces of type out and recover them after school. Apparently, Dave kept his stash of type from Junior High School. When in high school, someone got hold of the answers to the state trigonometry test. The answers were a,b,c,d multiple choice answers. Dave used his type to make up a cheater pencil. With a hammer, he tapped pieces of type corresponding to the answers into a wooden pencil — all the answers within two inches of pencil. Dave was so proud of his craftsmanship that he showed the pencil around school. I said to myself, "That guy is a proud and dedicated cheater!"

Unfortunately, those with the answers gave them to too many others, and our trig classes scored higher than any group in state history. There were more than a dozen perfect scores! This caused all hell to break loose with accusations flying. A large number of students confessed. Even many of the best students in the class cheated. But to have had a perfect score on a test that was well beyond what we learned? How smart was that?

Mr. Dzak

Our neighbor was a retired Polish immigrant. He was a quiet, kind man, short and stocky. You hardly knew that he was there, next door. He was very hard of hearing. He had two hearing aids. When the air was thick with humidity in the heat of summer, Mr. Dzak's TV would be blaring. This was before the age of air conditioning. For relief from the heat, doors and windows were wide open. On such days, we would sit on the front porch to get some air.

Mr. Dzak liked to watch professional wrestling. He got absorbed in the hero/villain psychology of the matches. At first, the villain would give a beating to the hero. Usually, this was through some kind of cheating—- like a low blow when the referee was not looking. The hero would eventually recover enough to lay into the villain.

From our porch, the wrestling match would be blaring. Then a deep-chested voice would well up through the din, well up to a crescendo, "Geeve it to um. Geeve it to um." The urgency of the shouts would bring smiles to our faces. Every time he would say, "Geeve it to um," we looked at each other and laughed. Then he would go silent for a while. Again, through the noise of the TV, his voice would well up, "Geeve it to um."

Dewey in the Conga Drum

Bison lived close to the university area. Surrounding it was a lively movie and nightclub district. It was next to a Jewish community and a black community. Local representatives of the beat generation lived and practiced their arts in that area. Bison was constantly talking about alternatives to being straightlaced. He asked if I wanted to go to a hip poetry reading. I joined him at his house, and we took a bus to the university area.

The reading was on a Sunday afternoon in a room behind a storefront. The store did not seem to be prospering. It was disheveled and dusty. It was closed on Sunday. We headed to the back room. In it there were a dozen or so folding chairs set up and a small area in front where the poet was going to read. Behind the reading area was a sizable window with wire reinforcement embedded in the glass. The window was dirty, but it let in some light. There were six of us in the audience — a bag lady, a sleeping guy, a good- looking couple, and us.

In the performance area, a large, muscular, black man stood. He had a form fitting T-shirt and otherwise West Indian dress. He had a shaved head and big circular earrings. He stood in front of a conga drum. Next to him was a shortish guy in a beret, vest, and jeans. I took it that he was the poet. With the drum player drumming, the poet started with verse about how obscure poets were and that what they were doing was for the real people in society. The real people were mostly the victims of impersonal business. As he read, he kept looking at the well-dressed couple. He probably knew them. He was certainly trying to impress them smiling at them in an ingratiating way.

His next poem was about Dewey the drum player. Imagine that Dewey was in the Conga drum. What did he see? When he looks up, he sees the skin of the drum. The poem went on about what Dewey saw from inside the drum. All the while, Dewey was smiling, playing the drum. Neither Bison nor I could quite get into putting ourselves inside the drum looking up at its skin, but we did think that the poem was humorous. The poet then pretended to make a false start on another poem. He said, "Once upon a girl, a guy had a time," er, I mean, "Once upon a time a guy had a girl." He glanced over at the well-dressed couple and smiled. Clever guy.

Pickles

Rodent's dad made homemade pickles. Rodent did not think much of his father's pickles. This was peculiar because we called him Rodent since he would eat anything. We figured that his dislike of his father's pickles must be personal. It had something to do with not wanting to encourage his father. His father was likable and enjoyed telling us about hunting dogs, cars, and pickles. Rodent's friends enjoyed his father, but we were well aware that his father had an easy time getting worked up. His voice would suddenly get loud and he would begin to stammer.

Since Rodent was an only child, his parents often brought up how he always had it too good. They talked about how other kids behaved and how good they were. This irritated Rodent to no end. They enjoyed lecturing him in front of his friends. We were their angels who were supposed to give Rodent something to live up to. Other kids always deserved high praise while he always fell short. His father gave us a pickle to taste. I said, "'Yum' these are Grreat!" This brought a big smile to Tom's father. "How do you make them?" "I will give you the recipe." "I don't know why Tom doesn't like them." Rodent was hopping around in circles on one leg.

I made pickles according to his recipe. First, I needed a crock. Bison had just bought a motor scooter. We drove to a second-hand store and with used crock in my lap, I held on for dear life as Bison sped to my house. I bought a peck of cucumbers, some dill, garlic, and some secret ingredients. Let the batch ferment for a while, and holla! Tasty pickles! I put them in jars lining the back of our refrigerator. I reported to Rodent's father that they came out well. Rodent didn't like the taste of them.

Don't Listen to That Atheist

We were looking for a place to play basketball. St. Jude's had a night during the summer where you could come and play basketball. The catch was that you had to attend the confraternity class first. We said, "OK we listen to the priest talk a while. There will be girls there. Afterwards, we will play basketball." Good deal.

The class was in the basement of the church hall with windows at the ceiling that opened onto the sidewalk. It was a muggy night and humid in the classroom. The room was full — about thirty young people. The priest opened with, "Are there any questions?" No one had any. The priest then said, "Let's review the catechism." He began in the first row with, "Who made you?"

A young girl replied, "God made me." I reacted badly to this. He was treating us like children. He was going to review what we had been indoctrinated with. I raised my hand, "How do you know that god exists?" He seemed to be taken aback.

He proceeded with an account that began, "The universe is like a big wheel with god at its center." I then said, "You are saying that god is in the wheel. I asked how do you know that there is a god to begin with?" He stumbled into the Trinitarian view. Again, I said, "You are saying god is in three persons. But how do you know that there is a three-person god?" He was exasperated, and went on to call on other kids who by now were interested in asking questions.

We went on to play basketball. We did not think anything more about the class. The next week we decided to go back again. We were a few minutes late. We were going past the windows near the sidewalk. Coming out of the room was this angry voice. "You should not listen to people like that atheist last week. He is a bad influence. God will punish him." I broke into a smile. As we entered the room, his face went pale. He would not look at me eye to eye.

Years after this incident and having studied a little philosophy, I realized that if the priest had come up with one of the classic arguments for the existence of god, I would probably have agreed with him. I would have thought it quite neat. Thomas Aquinas presented an argument from motion, that there had to be a first mover. It would be a first principle that got the universe going. This would have made intuitive sense to me as a teenager. Instead, the priest was caught with no argument. He kept assuming the conclusion that he needed to prove.

The priest should have encountered Aquinas' arguments in seminary. On the other hand, the classic arguments for the existence of god have well known flaws. He should have also encountered that in seminary. In the priest's defense, it would have been intellectually dishonest for him to trot out an argument that he knew to be flawed just to put one over on a teenager. Unless, that is, he obeyed the higher calling of trying to save my soul.

Bohemian Tears

My father and his brothers had a similar ecstatic look when they were having a good time. I saw this look on other relatives on my father's side. It was always a response to seeing people whose company they enjoyed. The look was amplified after my dad had a few beers. It was ever present when beer accompanied the music of his youth.

In our home music was important. My parents made sure that we had music lessons and pursued music as far as we liked. My brother had a gift for music. He could hear melodies on the radio and pick them out on an instrument. Mr. Koshla, our neighbor a few doors up, knew of my brother's talent and gave him his violin. My brother picked out the opening phrase of, "Now is the hour, it's time to say goodbye." It sounded good. The only problem was that my brother kept playing that phrase. And it was always short and the same.

My parents got sick of it. "Now is the hour, it's time to say goodbye." They asked him to learn another tune. He did not. "Now is the hour, it's time to say goodbye." The neighbors got sick of it. They asked him to stop. "Now is the hour, it's time to say goodbye." My brother didn't like the lack of appreciation. He decided to give up the violin for the accordion. He started a dance band. I was his drummer.

My father listened to recordings of Bohemian brass bands when growing up. He danced to local brass bands when courting my mother. He had friends who played in those bands. Some bands produced recordings that were sold in area furniture stores. The Bohemian brass band music was particularly sweet and flowing. Each piece had a legato section that would appeal to the richer emotions. The tunes were melodic, noble, simple, and emotional. Some of the recorded music with the largest and best-arranged bands was imported from Czechoslovakia.

Much of the imported music was written between the wars when Czechoslovakia was formed and lived as a free democracy. Anyway, when my Dad would hear this music, he would have that mellow look on his face. He would smile and his eyes would get glassy. Sometimes he teared up. I felt something like what he felt. I came to understand it as a kind of amber melancholy. It was a happiness tempered by life's weight. The shadows of the past never leave while the music presents a reality that is noble and good.

By the time I was in college, my dad did not listen to the old music any more. As a present, I bought him an imported recording. I thought that it would make him feel good. I thought it would make him nostalgic. He played it quite a bit and then stopped playing it altogether. I asked him why he didn't play it any more. He said, "The music haunted me. I could not get those melodies out of my head. I couldn't sleep at night. I needed for it to stop."

Chapter VII

Sipe's Spring Step

With athletics came the desire to get in shape. Some of us went to the YMCA where they had a weight room. I bought some weights that I used in my basement — the usual barbells and dumbbells. I made a lat machine with a cable, pulley, and water pipe system. Since I was interested in playing football, I wanted to develop my legs. I wore leg weights to school under my pants. I read the weight lifting magazines and tried to bulk up. I didn't have much of a chance to succeed because I had a medium to light frame. A big frame displayed muscles in broad fashion. Even with added muscle mass, I didn't look a whole lot bigger.

At the time, there were Charles Atlas ads in magazines. The adds included a cartoon that takes place on a beach where some big guy embarrasses a skinny kid in front of the girls by kicking sand in his face. A second cartoon panel shows what happened after following the Atlas program. The kid is now muscular and easily defeats the bully. Albie, a weight lifting buddy, said that the only effective exercise in the Atlas program was doing pushups between chairs. One hand on one chair seat, the other on another chair seat, and both feet on a third chair seat. You dip between the seats when doing the pushups. This got good results in developing the pecs (chest muscles).

One magazine article recommended the Rick Sipes spring step for developing the calves. You did it by changing the pattern of everyday walking. You would continue each step rolling up on your toes. So, you would step and then lift, step and then lift. This looks rather odd because as you walked, you would bounce up and down in a sprightly and affected way. I looked rather strange walking down the halls of the high school springing along. Friends asked what in the world I was doing. I told them that I was developing my calves. I was in training. I was doing the Rick Sipes spring step.

Thinking about Girls

Ditch, Stump, and Rick went to an all-boys Catholic high school. Rodent, Bison and I went to the public high school. Since elementary school, Rodent, Bison, and I went to school with girls. We had girls as acquaintances. We had girls as buddies. We had girls as confidants. We had girls as love interests. We did not think much about associating with girls in general. They were part of the social landscape.

Our friends at the Catholic high school seemed obsessed with girls. Whenever school was over, they would talk about stories that other guys told them about girls. The stories would almost always be about sex or sexual exploits. It seemed that there was a big reaction to the absence of girls. After school, guys with cars would cruise around the Catholic all-girls schools looking for action. Ditch commented that it must be neat going to school with all of those girls. Needless to say, Rodent, Bison, and I were able to introduce our Catholic buddies to a wide range of girls. Of course, many of them turned into their good acquaintances or friends.

Broken Ears

Tommy and Joey were twins a few years older than we were. They were fraternal twins, but they did look rather alike with similar build and similar faces. They lived up the street from Rodent, and he chummed around with them from an early age. Tommy had a fifty-six

Chevy. He had it primed a rust red color. He had no intention of actually painting it. The primer was cool. He had painted above the rear bumper, "The Wanderer." None of us at the time had our own car. So we begged the twins for a ride or we begged them to cruise and hang out.

I met a girl from the suburbs, and I tried to talk Tommy and Joey into providing transportation for a date to a party. They refused several times, but then agreed to do it for the usual gas money. We told them that they could attend the party too, but they said that they weren't invited and they didn't feel right joining in. Rick went with his date Carol.

Carol was a very sweet person. She was someone that everyone liked except the parents of boys who dated her. She was tall, and very full figured with big bazooms. She wore heavy make-up and had thick jet-black hair, hair-sprayed into a shiny mound significantly extending the top of her head. Hey, it was a style of the time. She wore tight skirts and tight sweaters. You got it. She was a sixteen-year-old who looked twenty-five and experienced. Rick made sure he brought Carol home to meet "the folks." Rick said that their eyes popped when first seeing her.

Well, the twins picked us up and took us to the girls' houses. I could imagine the girls' parents looking outside at the primed Chevy with the two big guys with black leather jackets in the front seats. We went to the party, and Tommy and Joey returned later to pick us up. We stopped for jelly donuts. We ate some donuts on the return trip setting the bag on the rear seat. When we got out of the car, we looked for the donuts. We could not find them. Carol then got up, and they were beneath her. Carol warmed them up considerably. Carol was embarrassed. We tried not to say how flat they were.

The twins were somewhat miffed that they spent their Friday night driving us here and there. So, Ditch, Rodent, the twins, and I shared some beers the next night while cruising. We had to pee. We were near a bridge that went over some sand pits. Joey pulled down the road under the bridge to let out some beer. When we were finished, I thought that I would make like a Hollywood actor and enter the backseat of the car in one motion. You know, hold the door handle with one hand, jump in, landing in the seat as I pulled the door shut.

It didn't work that way. I came down most of the way, but I caught my head in the door, closing the door across my ears. I dropped into the seat and oh did my ears hurt. I said, "I caught my head in the door and does it hurt." Everyone laughed hard. They could not believe that such a dumb thing could happen. I said, "I think I broke my ears." They laughed even harder. The next day, sure enough, I felt my ears and there was a ridge across both ears where the cartilage was broken. And were they black and blue! To this day, I can let you feel my broken ears.

Bison 's Luminous Curiosity

I thought I was curious until I met Bison. He had this vacuum cleaner of a mind, picking up information in corners that the rest of us did not realize were there. His friends also found his curiosity inspiring because he had an enthusiasm for life and the details about how it is lived. Once we went to the Sportsman's Show at the Cleveland Convention Center. The fire department had a display with a fire chief there to answer questions. Bill dug into finding out the lowdown. He asked what is the greatest danger to a fireman. Of course, I thought it was fires or maybe smoke.

The chief said it was when a number of trucks were speeding to a call. They went through red lights and stop signs. Their sirens were blaring so they couldn't hear other sirens coming. At the time, many firemen stood on the outside of the fire truck on a platform with hand railings. The chief said that most of the deaths in his time were from collisions and firemen being thrown from vehicles. Now, I would never have known that if it weren't for Bison.

Because Bison wanted to get to the bottom of things, I learned that there are always questions beyond the simple answers that satisfied most people. Needless to say, Bison put many of his teachers on the spot. He could be a royal pain because he insisted on honest answers.

Continuing questions, however, are dangerous. Anyone will quickly run out of expertise with repeated questions. This result did not enhance Bison's popularity with teachers. I always admired his forthrightness and sincerity in seeking answers.

Through Bison's interactions I learned about lasers when they were a scientific novelty. We also attended a political lecture where Bill put some Trotskyites on the spot. He was always on the lookout for things that were phony. He put me onto books like, <u>The Catcher in the Rye</u>, which included a theme like that. And then there was Salinger's <u>Franny and Zooey</u>.

The downside of all of this was that the absence of answers fed my skepticism and led to my dissatisfaction with institutions of many kinds. For example, if you tried to browse the physics or chemistry sections of the neighborhood library, you wouldn't be browsing for very long. Somebody forgot to include those sections. If you were interested in linguistics, there was a numerical gap where the linguistics collection was supposed to be.

Linguistics is a lost category of knowledge. Thousands of English teachers out there, but no ready sources on language research and the theory of language. What English teacher teaches English anyway? Almost all of them teach literature. Shortfalls of this sort led me to wonder, as a high school graduate, where in the world I could find the missing categories of books.

Later I became aware of the absence of any criteria for evaluating a subject. This is the sort of thing that would get a big reaction out of Bison. He was dogged in trying to get to the bottom of things. He suspected that the right questions were not being asked. What is good history? What is good psychology? What is good biology? What are the limitations of each subject? What might the future bring in each of them? Even if the libraries contained many books in a subject area, are these the best books? Are they consistent with each other? It was only a long way into college that I learned how to tackle such questions. In Junior High School, before I met Bison, I had anxiety and an intimation of being lost. Now I realize that I should have felt lost.

The Tool and Die Shop

Bison offered me his Saturday job when he could no longer do it. The aim was to clean the oil and metal shavings in and around the machines and floor of a tool and die shop. It was a small shop with about thirty machines and four employees. They produced dies for heater brackets in General Motors cars for example. The job was dirty, but it paid well. When I got everything cleaned up to the owner's satisfaction, I could go home.

I brought my lunch and ate with a nice guy named Harold. He was in his thirties. He was smart. He had a first-class technical education. He had a lot to say about life. One day at lunch, he told me that there was going to be a war that lasts many years. I asked him how he knew. He said that contracts had been let to other shops to make dies for military equipment used by soldiers in the field. The number and variety of such contracts indicated that the pentagon was gearing up for a long land war. He said that his shop turned down government work because they did not want to give kick-back. He said that not taking government work was hard to do because the profit margin was much greater than for other work.

Harold mentioned this in 1961. This was years before the Viet Nam War was talked widely about in the news media. This was seven years before the high point of troop buildup in the war. This experience made me all the more cynical about our government. When President Johnson committed hundreds of thousands of troops to Viet Nam, how were they able to equip those troops so quickly? They had been piling up material for years prior to the pretext that they used for starting the war.

Getting By and Moving On

I have to admit that I tried to earn <u>good</u> grades in high school—not excellent grades, just self-respecting ones. The nuclear arms race left me cold about my future. I had nuclear nightmares—waking up suddenly, in a sweat with my eyelids glowing red from the flash of a nuclear explosion. Of course, I didn't know that such nightmares were at the time quite common. I thought it was just me. I told my friends that I didn't think I would live to see 30 years. For that reason, I was not one to push for achievement on the academic front. Deferring the enjoyment of life was just not smart. I had to pack a lifetime into the present. I set out to have fun. I sought parties. I got good grades. I moved on.

While I wasn't academically aggressive, I still was irked that I couldn't get answers to questions that bothered me. We had no Internet, no computers, no one to give informed answers. So, for example, math classes lacked context for what we were studying. No teacher gave an overview of math. The textbook was mute on the subject. Libraries did not have books on the subject. How did current studies tie into the field of mathematics? No history of mathematics. No mention of the limits of mathematics. No ideas about what mathematicians are currently working on. No discussion of math as a live discipline. It was just that tenth grade was the time for geometry.

Anyway, I could go on with this carping, but I bring it up because I had no idea of the size of math. Is high school math, fifty percent of all math, 1 percent, or .1 percent? The attitudes of everyone who had been there, teachers, other students, parents, indicated that it got progressively more difficult as studies continued. Some of my questions were defensive. Fear was part of the math backdrop. As with most students, I took it as it came, and it didn't seem too bad. But what was it and what was it for?

I later learned that this was a Kafkaesque way to think. We were trapped in an endless bureaucracy of rooms and you moved from one to another with no sense of context or purpose. Some students liked math because teachers said they were good at it. I was not in that group. Even if I were, what were the teachers saying? What did they mean? It seemed like parental praise for the best hurdle jumper. I applied the same sort of thinking to my other subjects.

The Guidance Counselor

Every senior in the high school had a session with a guidance counselor. The aim was to talk about their future. I was in the academically talented section. I had a B plus average. I did fairly well on standardized tests. I read college catalogs in order to try to understand how college worked. My parents hadn't been to college. They could not advise me. Bison knew quite a bit about it. He answered many of my questions. The counseling session was welcome. I needed some guidance.

My counselor was an elderly woman named Mrs. White. She went over my record. She said that my grades were good enough to get into the major university in Cleveland — Western Reserve. She asked me how much money I had. I said that I did not have much — only what I could save from my Saturday jobs. She asked how much money my parents could supply. I told her that we were poor. Besides, my parents did not want to help me. They preferred to spend what little extra money they had on other things.

Mrs. White then said that the best thing I could do was not go to college and get a job! I was taken aback. I did not need a professional counselor to hit me with that one. I thought, "a pox on Mrs. White." I realized that this was one more area in which I had only myself to rely on.

A Bag of Dimes

Prom week ended with a trip to Cedar Point — a large amusement park on Lake Erie. I did not go to the prom. It seemed to be a rite of passage for the girls who were more interested in the event and their dresses than their dates. I also felt alienated from the faculty during high school. No teacher took an interest in me nor my attempts to accomplish something. I could not stand eating dinner with some of them at the prom. Rodent's feelings were similar. Rodent, Ditch, and I went to Cedar Point to have a good time in spite of the prom.

Our obsessive goal, of course, was to find girls. We decided to have a party in our hotel room. Throughout the day we would invite as many girls as possible. We scoured Cedar Point for interested parties. We quickly came upon three girls who asked us for a dime so that they could call their parents. They said that they were out of money with no way to call home. We felt sorry for them and gave them a dime. One girl was particularly distinctive. She had one tooth in front instead of two. Her one tooth filled the entire gap. She said that her boyfriend was in the Marine Corps. After they got the dime they disappeared.

As the day wore on, we saw them talking to loads of people, and it was always someone different than the last time we saw them. It appeared that their parents were not showing up to drive them home. Rodent approached them and struck up a conversation about them getting home. The short one admitted that they were not stuck but that they were having a good time asking people for dimes. She opened her large purse and pulled out a large bag of dimes — the size of a cantaloupe! I don't know if that was the day's haul or the week's but they had a lot of dimes.

After dark we went on a few rides and then back to our hotel room to get ready for the party. We had a radio and some refreshments. We discreetly posted signs leading up to the room. A knock came on the door. We thought that the girls had arrived. No, it was the house detective. We were not allowed to post signs in the halls. We waited for the girls to show. Rodent was the lookout. None came.

Marty

Most houses on our street had a front porch, and many people sat out in the summer and watched as people walked by. The front lawns were about twenty feet to the sidewalk. A five-foot tree lawn led to the street. The shade trees on the tree lawns were the dramatic feature of the street—— a high canopy of rich green. Up the street from our house was a family with children several years older than we were. The eldest son was about a dozen years older than I was.

I became aware of Marty at about the age of ten. He lived with his mother; his father was deceased. He had some illness that left him very thin. He had few teeth so his cheeks were sunken. In the summer, we would see him from our porch walking here and there, usually wearing a lime-green see-through shirt. He typically had his head down with a cigarette butt hanging from his lip. Nonetheless he always had a spring in his step. For whatever reason, through disability, bad luck, or choice, he did not work.

At times the police were after him. We did not know why. One day a squad car pulled up to the house. Two officers went to the front door. No answer. They walked to the back door and knocked. Meanwhile, Marty bolted from the front door. The police caught a glimpse of him and chased him. He eluded them by cutting through the yards. The next day, the police arrived. One went to the front door. One went to the back door. The basement window on the side of the house opened, and Marty bolted across the street. The police again were in hot pursuit. The plot was straight out of a Charlie Chaplin movie.

When my friends and I were in our mid-teens, we liked to sit around and talk into the night. Ditch had a smudge pot. Street crews would light such pots to mark a construction area or a hole in the road. It was spherical in shape, black, and contained kerosene. One night we were sitting around the smudge pot in Ditch's yard. Marty walked over and began telling us stories. He always spoke in a halting pattern, emphasizing certain words in a hard manner. "I used to BOX for BOY's in-DUS-trial SCHool," while he assumed a boxing stance. He said that some guy tried to fool with him. "He thought He was a Wise-guy but from around a Corner he MeT a lead PIpe." We were cracking up inside from Marty's stories, but we dared not laugh in a disrespectful way.

Marty presented himself as an authority on cars. One day a big and tall guy came by, he and Marty talked, and the guy drove away. At about seven o'clock on that hot muggy summer evening, the guy returned all dressed up in suit and tie. He was evidently going on a date. Marty popped open the hood of his car and began by taking out the air cleaner. He revved the car and tried to adjust the carburetor. After some time, parts were all over the place on the car and in front of it.

As Marty was pulling out parts and putting others back, the guy was getting hotter and uncomfortable. He shed his coat. Then he loosened his tie. Took the tie off. Rolled up his shirtsleeves. As each piece of clothing came off, I was in stitches. The piece de resistance was when darkness made work impossible, Marty looked for his flashlight. After some effort, he found it. He flicked on the light, and ta daa, there was this dim orange glow. It was so dim it illuminated nothing. The front of it could have been painted with orange paint. Finally, the guy was making signals that he had to go. Marty tried to put the car back together. After much effort, he had parts left over. He put these in the back seat! The car made this straining sound, and black smoke came from the tail pipe. No date for that guy that evening.

Chapter VIII

How to Breathe

Most of what occurs in our bodies happens in spite of us and that includes breathing. As an adolescent, I became interested in gaining control of my powers. I had begun reading a Yoga book recommended by Bison. In it there was a long section on breathing. I was shocked to learn that we can breathe incorrectly. Just like most things in our power, we can fall into bad habits. I thought that the section on breathing should be short. It was long.

What all could someone say about it? For starters, we use our abdominal muscles, diaphragm, and chest muscles to breathe. Most people are shallow breathers. Their abdominal muscles go in and out in short little spurts. This leads to fresh air entering only a small part of the lungs. With little exchange of air in the upper lung, toxins tend to accumulate. Over time, the toxins cause diseases such as lung cancer.

At the time I wondered if what they said was true. Does most lung cancer from cigarette smoking, for example, occur in the upper lung? Could vacating the whole lung with each breathe save many smokers from cancer? I set out to train my breathing. The Yoga book said that a breath should be in four parts. It should use all the muscle groups. Use of the diaphragm is of particular importance for control of the breath.

I practiced the techniques until they seemed to be automatic. I would watch others to critique their breathing. I concluded that most people didn't know how to breath, at least in the recommended Yoga way.

So Little Time, So Much to Know

After graduating from high school, I began serious reading that cast a wide net. I was trying to build a background in important topics not covered in public school. As my friend Sam said, "School often interferes with your education." I found that education through high school was narrow and biased in extraordinary ways. How this is so, is best left for another time.

I also ran into the brute reality that reading is time-bound. So many books, so little time. I tried to get my head around it. My cousin Bev's husband Russ was a reporter for The Cleveland Press, a major Cleveland newspaper. At a family gathering, I told Russ about my dilemma. He agreed that each of us can hardly scratch the surface of human knowledge.

Libraries are great and impressive. Human knowledge is on shelves in stacks—— all over the world, millions of books. I told Russ that if I read a book a week for the rest of my life, I would read three or four thousand books. A drop in the bucket—— a couple of library stacks at best. To make matters worse, I would remember little of it over time, let alone apply it to useful tasks. We face the great problem of selectivity. Every choice of a book to read means excluding a countless number of other books.

Much of my discussion with Russ had been building through high school. I got the creeping sense of just how little I could know. My best recollection is that my worry started with mathematics. My algebra text book had a dozen chapters with exercises. But what is algebra? How much algebra is there? Are there fifty text books of algebra, each getting more advanced than the last? Has algebra been developing for thousands of years? The public library and high school library had few algebra books and they seemed to cover only "first course" material.

As a sophomore in college, I visited the Case Institute of Technology campus and naively went to one of their libraries. In it I found thousands of books on chemistry. When I brought my visit up to one of my teachers, he blithely and blankly said, "Yes, there is a lot to be learned." He didn't get the emotional gravity of my visit. What is someone, some serious person, to do with their life? Get nowhere working through a small fragment of a subject? Who are we, if that is what we do?

The Bookworm

Bison had been admitted to a first-rate liberal arts college. Over the summer, before he set foot in a class, he was expected to have finished a reading list. It contained thirty-two books. Many were history books, some were literature, others biography, and a little science. Bison was impressed and somewhat daunted. He had not encountered such high expectations before in school.

I was about to attend a newly formed community college. There was no reading list. So, I copied a number of items from Bison's list and added some of my own. This would be my preparation for college. I had twelve weeks to read twenty something books. It was about two books per week. I planned to spend several hours per day reading.

As I became absorbed in my reading, I found it difficult to put a book down. I was also driven by my goal of finishing about two books per week. I had gotten a job painting trim at a chiropractor's office. The chiropractor's office was about three miles away. It took me forty-five minutes to walk there. I decided to try to read while walking to and from work. I found that reading while walking to be doable but required effort and concentration. I would walk the same streets to work each day. After a few days, I could sense my way down the sidewalks; parts of the walk became automatic.

Two girls in their early teens noticed me walking while being absorbed in a book. Sometimes they saw me doing this on the way home too. After a day or two, my reading bothered them. One of them said from their porch in a rather loud voice, "Bookworm! Look at the bookworm." On my return from work, one said, "Here comes the bookworm!" The other said loudly, "Oh, no. The bookworm's back." They were roughing me up, calling me a name. I paid them no mind and kept on walking and reading.

I didn't mind being called a bookworm. That's what I was. On the other hand, their emotion was criticism rather than praise. I sensed that they wanted to spoil my concentration. They wanted a response from me. They wanted me to say something to them. They didn't want me just to continue reading. I tried to change my route to avoid them. At times I still encountered them, and they continued calling out, "Bookworm."

Speed Reading

Pitchmen claimed that most Americans read too slowly. We could learn to speed read. In the advertisement, an actor would pretend to read. He would move his forefinger straight down the page of a book. This took all of a second. This was supposed to mean that he had read it. He did the same with the second page and then turned it. At that pace, he could cut through a book in less than five minutes. The ad suggested that we all had the potential to read more than a thousand words per minute. We could read all of those books that we wanted to read but just didn't have the time.

I didn't believe the ad. I did believe that I could read more rapidly. This would help me do well in college. I timed myself. Sure enough. I was a slow reader. I read just a little faster than I normally spoke. I went to a reading teacher. He had a machine. It had a moving slot. The slot framed a few words in a text. It masked the rest of the page. The idea was to slowly speed up the slot. This was to develop a new norm of faster reading. The trouble was that the teacher charged about the same amount of money as my college tuition for the fall semester. I declined his services.

I found a book called _Speed Reading Made Simple_. First it advised avoiding a pitfall like vocalizing what you were reading. Second, the aim was to pare down the number of eye fixations per line. Most of us read words. If you watch someone's eyes while they read, chances are that their eyes jump from word to word. There may be four or five eye fixations per line. The aim is to read phrases and clauses. So, instead of four or five eye fixations per line, you train your eyes to fixate only twice. This saves much time. Bison was interested in speed reading. He watched my eyes as I read and I watched his. Yup, too many fixations per line.

Instead of a machine, the book advised taking a three by five card and cutting a slot in it. The slot was a rectangle the height and half the width of a line of type. You moved the card left to right while concentrating on moving your eyes only when the card was moved. I practiced this way. Lo and behold, I doubled my reading speed! It was much slower than what the pitchmen claimed was possible. Speed reading helped me with the reading assignments I had as a freshman. With some courses, however, understanding ideas was more important than turning pages. I had to stop, think, and ask questions of what I was reading. This slowed my reading down, sometimes to a snail's pace.

An Epiphany

One day on a trip to the large record shop on Cleveland's public square, I had a life-altering realization. In addition to all the bins of records, there were storage shelves of records along the ceiling above the bins. The shelves were thirty feet long on two levels. They were all recordings of classical music. What in the world was all of that music about? I had no idea. It then dawned on me that there was the human heritage of serious music. I dove into that reality.

Giants Everywhere

Along with serious reading, I looked at the world afresh. I continued my aim to find out about life (see above What to Live For). I concluded that the aim of our short life is to understand what life is. I wondered what geniuses of the past had to say about it. As geniuses in whatever area of activity, they knew what I could never hope to discover on my own. I liked the idea that I could learn what the best minds understood about the meanings of life.

I had heard it said again and again that, "We stand on the shoulders of giants." Those who kept saying that, ended their discussion at that point. It was usually cited on some TV show on the arts where the narrator was trying to say something profound as a take-away. But wait narrator. Don't stop there. Which giants were you referring to and what was the view from their shoulders? Let's hear what the giants had to say. You're not going to tell us? What are we supposed to do, spend our lives wondering about what message they imparted? Start guessing about some message that was beyond our ability to discover on our own? Reinvent their wheel?

I looked for giants. I came up with some usual names. Shakespeare was one. Over two years, I attended a dozen of his plays at the Great Lakes Shakespeare Festival. He gave deep examples of social interaction and political intrigue. I later found that the problem with Shakespeare was that he never told us directly what <u>he</u> thought. The only exception was in The Sonnets where we got a glimpse. He was always presenting what some fictional character like Hamlet or King Lear had in mind. If all Shakespeare had to say was in quotations from characters in the plays, where was <u>Shakespeare's</u> philosophy?

For example, Polonius in Hamlet said, "This above all: to thine own self be true, and it must follow, as the night the day, thou can't be false to any man." The quotation was on posters in dorm rooms in the sixties. The trouble was that if a person with a character flaw was true to himself, he could often be false to others. If someone were a sociopath, he would genuinely be false to others as he pursued his own advantage.

The problem was with the self. Sometimes we should not be true to it. Shakespeare knew that because he gave examples of flawed characters in <u>Hamlet</u> including Hamlet himself. Shakespeare was <u>not</u> <u>claiming</u> what Polonius said. He had Polonius utter an unwise truism. Polonius, in the play, was just that sort of character.

Bach was another giant. I attended the yearly Baldwin Wallace Bach Festival. The scope and depth of Bach were beyond me. I was never quite sure I could enter Bach's devotional frame of mind. The music was sublime.

Picasso was a third giant. I saw his work in museums and one special show. I found that the meanings in many Picasso paintings required knowing events in his life. I needed to know them to attach meaning to his symbols.

Without a key to his symbols, I would not understand what he was trying to depict. This seemed egocentric and less than generous to his audience. He should have included a note by the title of each work that said the viewer needed to know certain biographical details in order to understand the representational aspects of the work. Nonetheless, for me, Picasso was the greatest graphic artist of the century.

Like with books being too numerous, there were so many giants and so little time to absorb their work. How do you identify the important giants? It occurred to me that little recognized giants built the current world of industrial civilization. What was their view and how did they do it? I also came to realize that regular sized people made the vastness of modern civilization possible. Perhaps that was the secret of our time. Genius had its place.

After a while, the idea of giants did not seem useful. Not only were there too many of them, but you needed a developed point of view to stand on their shoulders. I also realized that many meanings of life were best left for us to experience directly.

Manpower

The chiropractor assured me of work through my first summer out of high school. He reneged. I had three weeks left before college started. Rather than not earn money for these weeks, I decided to do day labor—- work for the company called Manpower. They were located on the outskirts of downtown Cleveland. That's where the old hotels, shelters, and Salvation Army housed most of their workers. Manpower gave you a check at the end of the day. Workers would come back when they needed more money. I guess the thinking of Manpower was that a portion of the labor pool can't hold down a steady job. Others can't get a steady job because they were fresh out of prison. If someone needed quick money badly enough, they would show up for day-work.

You had to get to the staging room by five in the morning. As employers called in requests for workers, the managers would point to people in the big room to come up and go on a job. Most jobs started at 7 AM. In order to get to Manpower at five, I had to wake up at 3 AM so I could walk to the bus stop and take the bus downtown.

At first, it worked out. My crew was sent to a manufacturer of printing machines. To get there, I had to chip in to someone with a car who would drive us to the job site. So, my expenses included bus fare, a brown bag lunch, and transportation to the job and back.

The driver was a young guy, about twenty, with a beater of a car. I sat in the front seat. It was loose. It sat on boards because the floor was rusted out. The seat was angled so that when I sat, I could only see the ceiling of the car. The car also had steering trouble. It lurched back and forth and vibrated violently as it accelerated. The driver couldn't go over 35 miles per hour. We were on the freeway poking along in the right lane. The driver had to hold onto the steering wheel for dear life or the car would veer to the right. As this was unfolding, I tried to see where we were going and what was going on. It was almost impossible.

The three other passengers in the car didn't say a word. They were half asleep. No one seemed to emotionally react at all. The lurching car didn't seem to matter to them. I didn't think we would make it.

We arrived at the job. We got out of the car on the circular drive, in front of the plant, and went in. Unbeknownst to us, the car died shortly after and the driver was told he couldn't leave the car there. He enlisted some help and pushed it into the parking lot. Upon arriving, one of our group was assigned to weeding the vast corporate lawn. Many dandelions. The remaining three of us were added to a crew of permanent workers to demo the interior of an old part of the factory. We were getting it ready for a different use.

We had a tractor with a forklift. One guy would stand on a flat on the forklift, be lifted to the ceiling, take a cutting torch, and cut some ironwork down. This gave off many sparks. The gas tank on the forklift leaked a pool of gas onto the tractor surface below it. I stood there watching those sparks. We had a fire extinguisher. As the gas caught fire, one of the guys would extinguish it. A little later, it would catch fire again, and it would be extinguished again. I kept my eye on it, judging the intensity of the fire for when to run. Fortunately, it didn't blow up.

I recognized one permanent employee as a famous full-back from the Holy Name High School football team. I asked him how much he made. It was more than twice what Manpower was paying us. It seemed in this case that the union rate went to Manpower and they gave us about half.

I learned that the older guys from Manpower were alcoholics. As they were paid at the end of the day, guess what many said they were going to do with the pay? One guy lived at The Salvation Army. His wife left him, and he had a breakdown. He smoked a pipe and looked as normal as anyone— kind of like a college Joe with the aspect of Hugh Hefner.

The driver of the car was a good guy with a tragic story. He ran away with a prostitute. She was wanted for unspecified crimes. She became pregnant, had his child, and was currently in prison. The driver lived with his grandfather who was raising the child. The way he put it, he had a few glory days with his lover, and the rest had been downhill. Last year, he was working a job and he injured his thumbs to the point where he could not grip with them. This made him unemployable except for outfits like Manpower.

I was assigned a different job in another area. Later that day I learned that our driver was injured. He had a big wrench. While trying to loosen a rusted nut on some ceiling ironwork, the wrench slipped and hit him in the eye. He had to leave work. His car was still dead in the parking lot.

As the day ended, I found a ride back to downtown. When we were passing the corporate lawn, there was this enormous pile of weeds, about four feet tall and almost as long as a semi. The poor guy assigned to do the weeding was in the blazing sun all day with his hand-held weeder, digging out those dandelions one at a time.

At Manpower, we collected our checks and went home. I spent

three more days working for them. On Friday, I got there on time and sat there until 7AM. They didn't call me up. No work for me. I was out my bus fare. I decided that unless they would guarantee me work, there was no point getting up at 3 AM.

Draft Test

A military draft existed since shortly after the Second World War. Part of the problem with the draft was that far fewer men were needed than the cohorts coming along. This was the beginning of the baby boom peak. So, perhaps twenty percent of young men were needed for military service. Because of this, deferments were given for a number of reasons.

In 1965, the Vietnam War was heating up. More men were needed, and large numbers of young men were enrolling in college to get an education deferment. The Selective Service Administration (SSA), the arm of the government that implemented the draft law, decided that many of these men were dodging the draft by marking time in college. They were thought to be token students who did not apply themselves to college level work. The SSA decided that the fakers should be found out and drafted.

They arranged a test. Any male college student who had lower than a B average would have to pass the test. If they failed it, they would be drafted. Needless to say, this caused a panic on many college campuses. One Saturday I was on campus and there was a long line of students sitting on the floor in a hallway waiting to enter the testing room. Students were walking up and down. The atmosphere was supercharged. The air was crackling. One student had a sign around his neck, "Score high or die." My grades were good so I did not have to take the test.

The Water Pollution Speech

I bumped into Rodent in a men's room at our college. He had three mason jars. I asked what he was doing. He said that he was about to give a demonstration speech on water pollution. One jar had some soil from the yard outside the building plus some tap water. Another jar was filled with tap water. The third jar he was about to fill with tap water and add a little liquid hand soap from the dispenser. He said that he would shake the first jar to point out all the sediment that settled out of the water. This was supposed to illustrate erosion. The tap water illustrated clean water, fit enough to drink. The third jar would dramatically show pollution at its worst. As he said, "As I take a pencil and stir the water, soap suds come to the surface and the class 'Oohs and Ahhs.' Pretty good, huh Boose?"

I said to Rodent that it sounded like a riot — good luck. Rodent was always right on the edge of not getting things done. That morning he came up with the idea, and he intended to pull off the speech with no rehearsal. He also thought that the teacher would give him credit for traveling around getting his water samples. One from a stream after a storm. One from a reservoir. One from the notoriously polluted Cuyahoga River. Later that day I asked him, "How did the speech go?" He said that the teacher had not believed where the water samples came from. The polluted water was just too soapy. You could imagine the concentration of soap that you would need in a river in order to produce suds like that!

Watching Airplanes Land

Throughout my youth, Cleveland Hopkins Airport had an observation deck. As a bit of entertainment, people would visit the airport, go to the observation deck and watch planes land and take off. This was a popular family activity on a Sunday afternoon. It was an alternative for a date on Saturday night. It was cheaper than a drive-in movie. There was something exciting, adventuresome, and modern about air travel.

Airports have long closed observation decks. To our current sensibilities, it would be a strange and pointless to go on a date to watch airplanes land and take off. There is no romance left in the activity. It would be like taking a date to the interstate to watch the trucks go by. Airports have become pedestrian, not special, utilitarian, and commonplace.

Responsibility and Wine Bottles

Bison and I met up while on vacation from college. He told me about the philosopher Jean-Paul Sartre and existentialism. The definition of self as tinker, tailor, soldier, or spy was just another kind of bad faith — a way to dodge responsibility for making authentic choices. Turn yourself into a role like that of a spy, and you did not have to accept responsibility for your choices. You could blame the role or the authority that set up the role. It seemed to make sense to me. Responsibility for self was a real burden. I thought it better to shoulder the burden than turn myself over to authority figures. I always had a deep anti-authoritarian streak in me.

Bison came to my college for a visit. We happened upon James Lorion, a college administrator. I asked Lorion, "If we know about some harm that someone is going to do, don't we have a responsibility to prevent it if we can? You know like Superman going around solving problems." Lorion said, "Sure we do." I then said that the more we find out about the world through media at all levels, the more of these harms become known to us. Do my responsibilities increase accordingly? Lorion said, "They do." I said that, "It would seem that I would have time for little else." Lorion said, "You don't want to be over extended." I said, "You don't have a choice once you know about the harm."

It seemed that the way to keep the burden on oneself manageable, would be to cultivate ignorance of others plight. Lorion said, "You shouldn't have a bad attitude about it." I asked Lorion, "Do our responsibilities for others in our community, city, region, state, country, and world keep mushrooming with our access to information?" He gave me a blank look. Maybe Lorion knew something we didn't. Bison and I were perplexed about Lorion's answers as well as the extent of our responsibilities.

The college was next to a cemetery where winos hung out. Most of them slept at the Salvation Army down the street. The winos hit students up for change as we walked to and from classes. Were the winos playing a role? Did we have any right to define them as winos? As we walked along the cemetery wall, the empty wine bottles, pint bottles, were always neatly standing up. Bison and I joked that it was important for them to maintain standards.

Verdi, Sausage, and Vino

At a piano recital, I recognized a guy from the neighborhood who was a few years older than I was. I had seen him at the community college. We struck up a conversation. His life was deeply based in music. His family was Italian. His father loved opera. His father made wine and homemade sausage. When I met Sam, his father was deceased, but Sam carried on family traditions. What impressed me was that Sam didn't just enjoy opera and good food. He knew an enormous amount about these subjects. I learned a lot from him.

In my pursuit of music, I checked out several classical recordings from the library each week. One week it would be Schubert Symphonies. Another week it would be Brahms chamber music. Another week, it would be Verdi operas. I played the records while I studied in the basement of my parent's home. During the Schubert symphonies week, I would be living through the Schubert melodies that ran through my head. As I was walking down the street, chunks of music would be playing inside of me. This happened during classes, at work, and before I went to bed. It seemed I was living my life through glorious creations of genius.

Sam and I with a number of other music lovers would convene in Sam's living room. His mother, sisters, and brothers would pass through the room. We all enjoyed them. A large number of relatives and friends would visit from time to time; it was a bustling household. After a while, we would settle into La Traviata, Il Trovatore, Rigoletto or the like and sip some wine. We would talk about the singers, their art, strengths, weaknesses, and careers. We took breaks to eat some pasta and sausage. Sam's mother always had some pasta and sauce at the ready. When the music got a bit loud, a neighbor would call the police. We would tone it down. For a while!

Joe Peeps

Sam, Jerry, and I went to eat at a favorite pasta house of Sam's. It was in the inner city. The sign above the storefront was, "Joe Peeps Never Sleeps." The restaurant was a tiny storefront with a stove. At the back of the store, several steps led up to a living area. There in front of a TV sat Joe. When he heard someone come in the door, he would come down to do business. Joe was in his sixties, short, nearly bald, of slight build, and he wore thick eyeglasses — like pop bottle bottoms.

The food at Joe's was good and inexpensive. He served homemade pasta and pizza. He made great Italian sausage sandwiches — you know, with fresh rolls, boiled white onions and green peppers. He charged so little for food that his profit margin must have been small. That day Jerry ordered pasta. Joe forgot to bring the shaker of Parmesan cheese. Joe always seemed to forget to bring the cheese. We began to suspect that Joe was trying to conserve his Parmesan cheese. Jerry asked for it. Eventually Joe brought it over.

Jerry started to shake out the cheese and little was coming out. The holes in the shaker seemed to be plugged. Jerry unscrewed the top of the shaker and tried to unplug the holes with his fork. He put the top back. Joe happened to be walking to our table. Jerry shook the shaker, the top popped off, and all the cheese fell in a mound on his spaghetti! Joe went pale. His eyes bugged out. He was visibly shaking. "My cheese, my cheese!" he said.

Invasion of the Calf Spotters

When I was a freshman and sophomore in college, I spent a lot of time in downtown Cleveland. One day I was walking along admiring the well- dressed business women and clerical workers. I noticed that one of them had a red oval spot on her calf. After that, I began to notice such red spots on other women's calves. The next day and for about a week, I saw dozens and dozens of women with red spots on their legs. They were always about the same size and almost always on the right calf.

I wondered what would explain the red ovals? Maybe one woman had a skin condition. But there couldn't be a plague of such conditions. Besides what skin condition caused such a neat hard-edged shape? It was also suspicious that the spots were on the calf only. Or were they? I couldn't see the rest of their legs. Maybe they had other ovals on their thighs? I did not ask. Placement of the spot on the calf was also perplexing. Why would it appear in the same place?

Maybe the spots were some kind of fashion statement. Maybe I should check Vogue Magazine to see if there was a red spot craze. I suspected, however, that none of them knew that they exhibited a red spot. I looked at lots of other people. No one seemed to be looking at the red spots. They were only impressing me. I brought up the calf problem to fellow students and my Mom and Dad. They had no good suggestions.

Was it done to them in the middle of the night? Was it some kind of diabolical act? Why was there only one spot per woman? Why did some women not have a spot? This left me puzzled. Big women, small women, and the ovals seemed about the same size. It was almost as if someone took a stencil and traced the oval shape. It might be aliens. That's it. Maybe some aliens were marking our women. They were being branded with a red spot. Pity the poor women when they got abducted!

Lo and behold the right explanation came to me in a flash! The flash, of course, was after spending far too much time and intellectual effort. It wasn't a skin condition. It wasn't a fashion statement. It wasn't alien marking. They didn't know they had ovals. What was it? They spent some time with their legs crossed — usually the right leg over the left knee! Mystery solved!

Taking the Bus

I took buses to college. The ride was usually uneventful. One day loud music came from the back of the bus. I did not look back. At first, I thought that some nut was blasting the radio. After a while I realized that it did not sound like a radio. This was before the era of boom boxes. This was the era of modest transistor radios. Anyway, it couldn't be a radio. The songs came one right after another. There was no dialog. No commercials. When I got up to exit the bus, I saw what was going on. A kid in the back seat had a 45 RPM record player that worked on batteries. He was spinning discs, playing disc jockey!

One day a nice young girl sat in the seat behind me. I was reading over some notes from a class. The bus was nearly empty. A young rather hip looking guy got on the bus, saw her, and sat next to her. He appeared to know her. I was trying to study but the bus was quiet and their voices were unmistakable. He was trying to make time with her, and she was resisting his advances. He said, "Why don't you go out with me?" She said, "I already have a boy-friend." He said, "Isn't it about time that you got yourself a man!" She said, "I don't think that I'm ready for one of them yet."

Chapter IX

A Steel Maker's Dawn

I needed a summer job. Dad worked in a steel mill but did not have the sort of influence that could get me a job there. I went to the Ohio Bureau of Employment Services. A sign on the board said, "Berry pickers needed." I asked about the job. The counselor said that I did not want to work with that group. He called a few days later. He got me a job in a steel mill.

In order to work in the plant, I had to buy fireproof clothing and steel-toed boots. This consumed nearly a week's pay. I worked for a week. There were cut backs. All the new hires were to be laid off. But they offered us an opportunity. Workers were needed in the office. To land the job, you had to pass a typing test. I was the only one who passed the test. I worked in the office as a summer replacement until vacations ended. Then they transferred me to the electric furnaces. I had to work swing shifts.

My turn at night shift required an adjustment. Starting at eleven pm was o.k. But I was not prepared for sunrise. Dawn in the valley of steel mills was a spectacular sight. Glowing furnaces, glowing steel ingots, and incandescent lights in a seemingly clear night gave way to the sun's rays laterally piercing layer upon layer of smoke and dust in reds, pinks, browns, purples, and grays. I was amazed at the enormous quantities of smoke and dust that became visible at dawn and then became largely invisible as the sun rose in the sky. The appearance of the mills at night was as close to what an underworld environment must look like. Nothing appeared natural. The stars and moon were occluded. The mill yard was an endless stretch of cinders. The only living things were the workers.

Cutting Through Scrap Metal

The electric furnace crew was strong and silent. The noise was amazing and frequently so oppressive that you had to be two inches from someone's ear, shout, and then have him turn to look you in the face to acknowledge that he heard you. This sort of an environment did not encourage conversation. The furnace men learned to communicate through simple gestures and facial expressions.

Each batch of steel was called a heat. The nosiest time was at the beginning of a heat. Three electrodes, the size of thick telephone poles, were lowered onto scrap metal to begin cutting it. The noise and vibration was so great that the whole gigantic building vibrated and swayed. Once a burly truck driver was standing in the building when a heat began. As the cutting started, he ran from the building. He later said that he had never heard noise so loud and jarring. It scared him.

Material Handling

In the electric furnace crew, I was the low man. I was given odd jobs. I had a job on the crew only because the union required a certain number of men in the crew. Without the union requirement, Management would probably have had much smaller crews. My official job title was "Material Handler." Now that's self-explanatory! When the odd jobs ran out, I was to sweep the floor with a push broom.

The furnace building was about one hundred yards long and about seventy-five yards wide. The ceiling was about fifty feet up. Batches of steel were prepared by adding material to the furnace such as nickel ore and limestone. There were several large cone shaped piles of material on the floor. A guy with a frontend loader would scoop up the right amount and dump it into the furnace. The scooping and dumping phase kicked up large clouds of dust. The intense ceiling lights made the dust show up like layers of clouds.

All day long the dust rained down on the floor. The accumulation rate was rather uniform. I would sweep the floor by starting at one end of the building. By the time I reached the other end, the floor behind me would be covered by about an eighth of an inch of dust. I did an about face and swept the other way. I did this back and forth all day long. Needless to say, it was very frustrating. On night shift, the foreman would let me take breaks from sweeping. All he cared about was that the floor looked swept for the next shift. During the day, however, the "white shirts" walked around. You had to look busy. So, sweep I did.

Frozen Russian History

When I entered college, the cold war was a bleak reality. The Soviet Union was preeminent in space exploration. I thought that it would be beneficial career-wise to know more about Russia. I took courses in the Russian language and Russian History. My Russian history teacher, John Zubal, was a character. He appeared very conservative — military haircut, very plain wash pants, white shirts, black ties, and sport jackets. He drove a Checker car; they were the original taxicabs.

His class met at eight in the morning. This was a deadly hour for a teacher. The class entered half asleep. The old steam heat and florescent lights were enough to cause many a Russian history devotee to nod off. There was also the danger of whiplash. As you fell asleep sitting up, your head would drop and you would suddenly snap it up so as not to fall over. Well, our teacher solved that problem. He would open the windows as wide as he could before class. In the winter, snow would be blowing in. The wind would be bitter cold. The temperature dropped so you could see your breath. The class would sit there shivering. Zubal then entered the room, closed the windows and started the lecture.

Ah Ha! A "B"

Our Assistant Dean for Student Affairs at the community college, wanted to keep grade point averages as high as possible. When helping students fill out their class schedules, he tried to balance challenging academics with other offerings such as soft sciences and physical education. He also did not want students to take more than a full load of courses. He was correct that thorough preparation required a number of hours per course. This limited the number of courses that a student could take realistically.

As a second semester freshman, he tried to keep me at a full load. But I had plenty of time to study, and according to the tuition policy, courses beyond a full load were free. So, I insisted on taking eighteen hours. He told me that I would not do well and that after I did not do well, he would cut me back next semester. He said that my grade point average would tell the tale. Well, I earned five A's and a B that semester. I was ready for him. I went to schedule my next semester.

Dean Swank remembered me, but I could tell that he hadn't looked at my file yet. I started talking about taking another overload. He reacted in reflex saying that it was not advisable. Then he said, "Let's look at your record!" I couldn't wait for him to see my grade point average. He looked at my grades and paused a little. He put his hand on his jaw and said, "Ah! Ha! A "B." I thought that his response was too much! But I did have an easier time getting the schedule I wanted.

Conventioneering

Rodent was back from college for the weekend. He asked if I had done any convention crashing. I said, "No. But I am ready for a break. Let's do it." We went to downtown Cleveland. The first step was to cruise the hotels to see what was happening. We started at the biggest hotel of the time. I was headed for the lobby when Rodent advised that we enter via the parking garage. He said that we didn't want to attract attention from the front desk. He then located a service elevator. We went floor to floor until he saw some steel shelves with used dishes, bottles, and linens on them. He grabbed an empty liquor bottle and winked.

A way down the hall, he saw a "Wet Paint" sign attached to the wall with masking tape. He stuck it on his chest. He said that the first aim is to look like you belong. We rounded a corner. He acted drunk. To everyone we encountered, he said, "My bottle's got a hole in it. (while turning the empty liquor bottle upside down). Where's the party?" We got the word on what conventions were in the hotel and where they were. We bumped into a guy with a chest full of buttons. Rodent said in a tipsy voice, "I lost my button. Can I have one?" The guy gave him a couple of buttons. With buttons on, Rodent then said that we were in!

The first convention was for Scottish police. We saw the kilts. We heard the bagpipes. They were in a major ballroom. We tried to enter but the guy at the door stopped us. I peeked into the ballroom. Everyone was much older than we were, and most were in Scottish outfits. We gave up on the Scottish police convention. We moved on to a writers' convention. They met in a largish room. We went in and struck up some conversations. We quickly concluded that the group was too small, the guys were dressed in sport jackets, and they didn't look like they were having a good time. We left.

We got on an elevator. Sitting on the floor was a guy dressed in something like a pirate costume with a machete on his belt. He had pushed the buttons for all of the floors. He said that he was riding the elevator endlessly. "I am not going to find a party. A party is going to find me." Rodent said that some conventions turn into wild parties that break out of their rooms. I said that we should keep looking.

We heard that a science fiction convention was meeting in the main ballroom. As we got closer, we found people in all manner of science fiction costume: people with antennas sticking out of their heads, green people, the bride of Frankenstein, and even some trekkies. When we arrived at the ballroom, the crush of people had left. We missed the big party! Tables were overturned. Food was on the floor. Vomit was on the rug. People were sitting on the floor drunk and dazed. The room was a wreck.

We got a play-by-play description of the party from Count Dracula — a Bela Lugosi look-alike. I noticed that some of the conventioneers were twelve to fifteen years old. I asked them where they were from. They were from California, New York, and Atlanta. Their parents had put them on airplanes to Cleveland for the science fiction convention!

It was after eleven o'clock when we left the hotel. Rodent then said, "Let's head over to the Manger Hotel to see what is going on." I said that I had to work on Sunday and besides, I had much homework to finish.

Using Words to Change a Tire

The student professed being an intellectual. He said that his demonstration speech would be intellectual. I thought that this was vain. Why should anyone bring up how great they are? He was strawberry haired and somewhat cherubic. He had lots of freckles. I realized that anyone who trumpeted that he was an intellectual was probably very insecure in many ways including intellectually.

His speech was on how to change a tire. He said that you get the jack, spare tire, and lug wrench out of the trunk. You then loosen the lug nuts and take the wheel off. At this point the class began to titter. As he said that you should put on the spare and replace the lug nuts, the class erupted in laughter. He did not realize he said that all of this was done without jacking up the car. His face was red. He did not know what everyone was laughing at.

Half-Concerts on the House

As a college freshman, I became a regular at Cleveland Orchestra concerts. Under conductor George Szell, they did great art and established a reputation around the world as a very fine orchestra. At the time I was trying to figure out what great art was and the orchestra gave me living examples. Szell's concerts were often sold out. If you arrived when the box office opened and the concert was sold out, there were a number of standing-room-only tickets at a bargain price. My friends and I aimed for standing-room-only.

My studies occupied most of my time. Many weeks, I studied through Saturday night but it was good to get away to a concert when I could. I often went with my friends Joe, Jerry, and Sam. On some nights, the concert wasn't sold out, so the box office would not sell standing-room tickets until the remaining expensive tickets were sold. The price was out of reach for us. We went home. Other times, the standing-room tickets sold out so quickly that we were left out. In the latter case, my buddy Joe figured out a way around the problem.

Instead of going home, we would have a cup of coffee at a nearby restaurant until we thought the intermission was nearly over. We would then stand behind the big columns by the front doors of the hall. In winter, it was mighty cold waiting for intermission to start. When the swarm of people exited to smoke cigarettes, we would put our coats on our arms and walk in. We would join the standing-room crowd at the back of the main floor. I guess none of the ushers thought that anyone would come to the second half of a program. No one seemed to look at us in a suspicious way. After the strategy worked so well, we would sometimes study into Saturday evening, and then head to the hall to catch the second half of a concert.

Big John

I had a psychology teacher who liked to tell stories. We called him "Big John." He talked about his time as a coal miner in Pennsylvania. During the Korean War, he served on the lines. He was wounded. He had facial reconstruction to prove it. He stayed in the military for some years. He spent time teaching in a public high school. He spent a number of years out west working in the national parks. He taught a number of years at a small liberal arts college in Indiana. After getting married he moved to Texas where he taught for some time at a public university. John had a special point or lesson to tell about each phase of his interesting life.

At the time I took copious notes. My note taking was to some degree automatic. I wrote down what the teacher said without reflection.

Later I might go back to the notes to cull out what was not important. About three quarters of the way through the term, I began to smell something fishy. The years that John just mentioned working on a fishing boat put him well over the top. I quickly went through my notes jotting down the number of years that John said he spent doing this, that, or the other thing. He was at least 87 years old!

The Cop and the Cognac

My friend Joe Rubino had a Corvair, the car that Ralph Nader said was not safe at any speed. That means that the car was dangerous even when parked! One day our group in the student union brought up the exposition in Montreal. Joe was game, so we set out in the Corvair. The engine was air- cooled. It sounded like a loud rattling air conditioner. This was numbing with the top down on a fourteen-hour drive.

To save some money, I packed some food along with a half empty bottle of cognac. We reached the Thousand Islands area of New York and were about to cross the border. We pulled into a park to eat a sandwich. Joe brought up the fact that we had to pass through customs, and one thing customs officials cared about was alcohol. Was it safe to bring in the cognac?

The park was rather empty. It was in a highly wooded area with a stream. A cop then pulled up alongside of us, and we struck up a conversation. Joe decided to ask him about crossing the border. The cop said that we had nothing to be concerned about. They would ask a few questions, and we would be on our way. I brought up the fact that we had the half empty bottle of cognac. The cop said that they probably won't search the car but that if we got caught, especially with a half empty bottle, our trip would be derailed.

I said that it would be a shame to waste the cognac. "What are we supposed to do, pour it on the ground?" The cop did not think that we should do that; it would be a waste of good cognac. The cop had the ideal solution. Let's drink it! As we passed the bottle around, the cop told us about north country — that people in north country kept things neat and orderly. He said, "Blacks don't like north country because it's too cold." He said that he did not see many blacks in the parks and that besides, they quickly learn that they can't do what they did in the city "up here."

So, we learned a little about some attitudes in north country. The cop had given us the impression that he had never been to an urban environment. He had the fears and prejudices that go along with such a lack of experience. We left a little light headed and probably beyond the legal limit. At least we didn't have to spill out the cognac.

"Botchie" The Pro

Joe helped me get a summer job at the elevator company where he worked. I was assigned to be a helper for a lead employee named Joe Potash. He was a Korean War veteran with a large scar that covered most of his head. I watched him and took his advice when learning the ropes. His key advice was to do the jobs that the foreman needed to get done, to help the foreman save face. Secondly, work at a pace that doesn't kill the job. When foreman Ernie was around, you worked. When he was gone, you didn't work much. If we ran out of work, somebody would be reassigned or maybe even laid off.

Ernie would often check the men's room for slackers. This was easy to do. It had no stalls, just toilets. The toilets didn't have seats. You had to sit on the cold china or try to hover over it. Toilet paper was of the lowest grade, coarse, rough, and gray in color. No privacy. No comfort. I took it that management didn't want employees hanging around the men's room. Employees thought the company was cheap and disrespectful.

When Ernie was not around and not much needed to get done, Joe took a set of blueprints and went on a tour for an hour or two. He would visit friends throughout the six floors of the large factory. So long as he carried the prints, it was unlikely that anyone would ask him why he wasn't at his station.

The long pauses between work sessions were filled with conversation. I noticed there was a guy a couple of stations over who was always working. I commented about it to Joe. He said, "Naw, he's not working. He's a pro." I didn't get what Joe was trying to say. Of course, that guy was working. I'd been watching him work for a month. I thought that if anybody was working, that guy was. I thought that maybe Joe just didn't take to a comparison between our way of working and "the pro's" way.

The worker was John "Botchie." Joe said they called him that because he always messed up a job. The foreman knew better than give him something important to do. So supposedly John was busy all day doing a job that he couldn't ruin. What do you think of that?

Botchie was an immigrant from Eastern Europe. He was about sixty, short, stocky, had a gravelly voice and almost always smiled with a wide Teddy Roosevelt grin that showed an impressive row of teeth. He was the picture of a little old man, like an old cobbler, donning his shop apron, hunched over his work. His work station had everything labeled, and he was neat. Whenever the boss would pay a surprise visit, he would always find Botchie working.

On the way out the door after work one day, I talked to Botchie. He had the worst attitude toward the company. Not that he was angry. He spoke quietly and expressed his bad attitude through that broad smile and all of those teeth. He said that he didn't want to give the company anything if he could help it. I didn't get his point but it seemed to jibe with Joe's opinion about him.

As the summer wore on, I heard some stories about Botchie. He prepared panels for elevator cars. The wooden ones had to be sanded smooth. The panels were placed on saw horses. Botchie would stand over a panel with his sand paper covering a block of wood. He would sand a little, take a look, sand again, walk around the panel, go to his bench, take a rag and wipe the panel. He looked careful and professional checking the work for imperfections. He would do this on the same panel for long stretches. Once Ernie caught him with the sand paper turned upside down on the block. He was only pretending to sand. He was using the paper side of the sandpaper. He was doing nothing to prepare the panel.

A similar Botchie story was when he was supposed to take a wood plane to the sides of a panel. A wood plane was used to take shavings off of a panel. The idea was to flatten an edge, bevel an edge, or eliminate bumps. The blade on the plane was adjusted beyond the base of the plane, the thickness that you wanted to effectively remove from the panel in one swipe. Botchie was planing away for most of a morning. The problem was that the blade was not set. He was pretending to plane. He was taking off no shavings.

Around August of that summer, Ernie got frustrated with Botchie, and wanted him to produce something. He gave him an important job. He asked him to cut some panels on the table saw. The panels were of high-quality wood. The stack he worked on were worth, in today's money, about twelve hundred dollars.

The word spread quickly throughout the shop that Botchie had cut all of them too short. They had to be scrapped. What was Ernie thinking? At that point I knew what "pro" meant. He did as he was told. He was a model employee, flawlessly obedient. Nevertheless, the employer got no output.

Later that day, I saw Botchie at his station. His eyes caught mine. He smiled with that Teddy Roosevelt grin and winked at me.

Herman the German

At the elevator company, the American workers adjusted work to the job. Don't give management a reason to reduce hours or reduce pay. Immigrant workers clustered in their nationalities and developed their own work strategy. It usually was that you gave the employer a day's work for a day's pay as defined by the worker. The boss couldn't get more out of them.

The exception to all of this was Herman the German. He had one of the worst jobs on the floor. He worked in the glue room. He glued wood panels into laminated sheets. He applied veneer. The panels were used in fabricating elevator cars. The glue fumes in the glue room would set you back. No one liked going in there.

When the horn blew at the beginning of the shift, Herman started work and he would work with gusto until lunch. He would resume with the afternoon horn and continue with gusto until the shift was over. He would be exhausted at day's end. He told me in broken English, "I take job from company. So I do job." The other workers, American and ethnic alike, thought that Herman was crazy. The fumes had gone to his head. He was a real company guy.

The rest of us got paid the same as Herman. Why bust our backs? Work to save face and stay out of trouble. When we were killing time, time slowed down. The day seemed endless. All the while Herman was just working away. Later in school I learned that German culture includes a strong sense of duty. If the duty was to do your job, you needed to work to fulfill your duty. You would work not for pay. You would work not because you needed to work to keep your job. You would work, like Herman, because you "ought to." It was a matter of morality.

Why Have A Teacher

I had transferred to Case Western Reserve University as a junior. I didn't shy away from difficult courses. They were about what I would have trouble learning on my own. If I could learn a subject on my own, I didn't need a teacher. But in needing a teacher, the learning curve was often steep. I was trying to build a background.

Most of my teachers, however, were aloof. They didn't want to interact. I watched them at a distance. I took from them what I could. I learned much about what I didn't know that I needed to know. I discovered from them how far I had to go to understand and work in a field.

Eventually I decided to major in philosophy. I realized that to be competent, I needed to be able to read difficult and technical literature. I took courses that prepared me for this. I didn't take courses to improve my grade point average or that just offered interesting information.

In spite of challenging studies, I was an honor student. I was not at the top of my class. I thought that in the longer run of life, what mattered was what you knew and could do. At the time, I didn't care much about cultivating who I knew or how to work the system. I guess to get by in life you needed to care about both priorities. I favored knowing things.

My friend Jerry majored in mathematics. This was the Jerry who spilled Joe Peeps' parmesan cheese (above). His father was killed in World War II. He lived with his stepfather who was a construction worker that often traveled. When visiting his home, I was standing by the kitchen sink. He said, "Get off of my bed." The patch of worn-away linoleum in front of the sink was where he slept. Their rental unit was small. He had been sleeping on the floor for years.

Jerry earned D's in math in high school. He told me that at that time, he just didn't care about school. He failed calculus at our community college. He took it again, liked it and earned an A. He majored in math and did very well. Jerry had strong intuition for math. He got a plum fellowship to do graduate work at the University of Indiana.

We met up once when he was home for vacation. He told me that there were certain math books that he would like to be able to read one day. He sought teachers who had competence with that material. Jerry was right on target. He was setting up a meaningful future and a high quality of life. We were often on the same page.

Gas for Around Town

Rodent helped me buy a TR3 sports car. It was several years old. It was missing a grill. It had a fresh coat of paint. Rodent said that the transmission was good. He said that was the key to buying a used sports car. He knew quite a bit about them. For minor parts, he took me to a junkyard. It was important to know how to scavenge a junkyard for parts and then what to say to the owner to get the parts practically for free. I worked on the car. Rodent helped me. It was my pride and joy.

One weekend, Rodent picked me up in his MGA. We went to his university to meet some of his fraternity brothers. At the time Kent State University had the reputation for being a party school. In the neighborhood, the saying was, "If you don't want to go to college, go to Kent." Along with his sports cars, partying, studying, and generally having a good time, Rodent collected animals from area parks. He kept them in the fraternity house. I saw his aquariums with bass and bluegill in them. He said that at one time he had quite a collection of cages, but he had to give up the furry animals because the fraternity house became infected with fleas. Yew! The house had to be vacated and fumigated. While this was going on, Rodent slept in his car parked behind the house.

College students were often broke. Rodent and his fraternity brothers tried to find ways around things. As we cruised from bar to bar, Rodent stopped at closed gas stations. At the time, a gas hose would have a loop in it. It would come out of the side of gas pump, loop down, and then back up to the pump handle. The loop held about a pint of free gas. We put the nozzle in his gas tank and then lifted the loop to empty the gas from it. The gas in the loop was normally no extra cost for customers. You would get the last customer's "loop gas" and the next customer would get yours. Unless! Unless, a Rodent was going around town emptying the loops, getting gas for free.

Given a Test

The Viet Nam War was expanding. The number of U.S. troops deployed was well on its way to half a million. The university was a hotbed of revolt. Most of the philosophy faculty, however, were living as middle class professionals. The war was a sideshow to their lives. Then they hired Fred Newman. He was anti-war, a Marxist, and unconventional. He was tall with a long beard, and always wore the same clothes—- jeans and his favorite worn sweater. The handful of philosophy majors at CWRU signed up for his class in the philosophy of language.

Fred thought the grading system was unnecessary. We're all to get A's, now let's get busy doing some philosophy. A heavy stress at Case at the time was the small number of A's given per class. Out of a class of 30 students, there might be 2 to 5 A's. B's were very common. Word got around to the chairman of the philosophy department that Fred was not going to give a final exam. After all, what's the point? Everyone was going to get an A.

The chairman and Fred had a collegial discussion, according to Fred, that the college rules required a final exam. So damn, being the all-team-player that he was, he had to give one. We took it that we didn't need to study for it. The major activities of the term involved working with us individually in writing a term paper. Lecture sessions were free-flowing inquiries into issues in the central literature. What could the exam cover?

His exam was a philosophical crossword puzzle. I kept it. It has 29 items. The questions were clever. "That from which norms emerge." Answer: action. "Everybody, what is everything?" Answer: contingent. "That being greater than which no being could be misspelled?" Answer: OGD.

Needless to say, I puzzled over a number of the clues. That was what I was supposed to do I know—— find it puzzling. I thought I understood Fred's wit and way of thinking, but I got only about half way through it. But that didn't matter. After passing the exam out, Fred posted the answer key on the wall and left. He had to give us an exam. So, he gave it to us.

Fred Newman left a mark on the student body. He starred in an anti-war play dressed as a general that kept giving orders to bomb everything. At the request of our undergraduate philosophy club, he debated a Jesuit philosopher from a nearby university.

The last I heard of him was in The New York Times. He formed a leftist political party. In being interviewed for the Times article, he stated something like this up front. Given the principles of his organization he could not accept donations from the Ford Foundation or major corporations. Fred was graciously turning down offers that would never come to him! That was Fred Newman.

Marty P. and Charm

Among our group of commuter students was an older guy, about twenty-eight. He returned to school after military service. He spent his tour in Korea. While in the army, Marty got a cushy job that allowed him to live off base. He spent his pay living in a hotel. He had lots of girl-friends. He made lots of guy friends. They partied a lot. Marty was a talented story-teller. He rhapsodized about hotel life. Every need was taken care of. You could get all the service you needed; you just had to know how to slip the quarters into palms of the bellhops and room attendants. Quarters? You won't get much service for quarters today. In the 1950's, a quarter was a good tip.

Marty was a history major. He loved the era of Louis XIV in France. He believed that the world was your oyster if you knew charm and manners. The French aristocrats knew how to behave. The counter culture of the 1960's appalled Marty. He said that one student took off his sandals in class and picked his toenails. Yuk! Anyway, Marty asked if I wanted to try a hotel bar in downtown Cleveland. It was called La Cantina. Not very original.

In the middle of the afternoon, we went for cocktails. A couple of Manhattan's and we would be set. The bar was very dark. The waitresses wore one-piece outfits with mesh stockings up to their hips and high-heeled shoes. It was sort of a take-off on the Playboy bunny. We got our drinks and began to talk about history.

Behind us were two women and one guy. The bar was quiet and Marty and I couldn't help but hear what was going on. We took it as a distraction to our conversation. Anyway, the women were friends, and the guy seemed to know them but not very well. I gathered that the women were guests at the hotel. The guy started trying to make time with one woman. She did not say very much. Then he started on the second woman. "Jean, Jean I love you so much. I will follow you to the ends of the earth. I will stand on the highest mountain and call your name." When I was about to get up, I glanced at them. The woman was quite plain looking. She seemed disinterested. Her affect was flat. Marty and I guessed as to what in the world they were doing. I asked Marty, "What does that have to do with charm? The court of Louis XIV?"

Chapter X

The Peace Train

Up to then, I had been to New York City only once. I marched in the great 1967 peace rally to end the war in Viet Nam. I was a junior at Case Western Reserve University. The industrialist Cyrus Eaton donated a train to all students who wanted a free ride to the march. Eaton's corporation owned the New York Central Railroad. The train was packed with students and working people who wanted to see an end to the war. By my count, the march drew well over two million people—-an endless stream of people from one o'clock in the afternoon till dark. The terminal point was the United Nations Plaza. By the time my group reached the plaza, it was full and I had to go my way. I had to miss Martin Luther King's speech.

At about eight o'clock, I made my way to Times Square. There on the moving light strip that flashed the news was something like, "March brings smaller than expected crowds. Only 430,000 people attend." I was incensed. The news establishment had under-reported the size of the march. They were partisans for the war.

When I returned to Cleveland, The Cleveland Plain Dealer diminished the march presenting pictures of hippies, a guy with a banana peel on his head, and kids burning draft cards. Where were pictures of the police units of Scottish bag pipers, veterans against the war, and trade unionists?

Swimming Through Plastic

I wanted to return to New York City to take in the arts. My wife to be, being an artist, was also interested in visiting the major New York art museums. We flew in and took in The Met, The Guggenheim, The Museum of Modern Art, and The Whitney.

The Whitney visit didn't take much time. At its midtown location, the Whitney building was a vast open space with fifty-foot ceilings. The show on view was of gigantic I-beam sculpture. This was where the sculptor welded together I-beams in various geometric configurations. They were interesting and certainly dominated the space around them. I could have invented social meaning for them, but I didn't. Industrial sculpture did not draw me in at the time.

We walked a few doors up from The Whitney, and we saw a large store front that contained an installation of experiential art. We couldn't see in and there was a somewhat pricey admission charge. We were dubious, wondering whether it was a scam intended to lure rube tourists. After going back and forth about it, we decided to give it a try. Upon entering, we were told to go single file and follow the big yellow footprints on the floor. We were instructed to look toward the ceiling for exit signs if we should begin to feel claustrophobic or panicky.

There was no way to tell the size of the room. The space was densely filled with strips of dry-cleaning bags hanging from wires along the ceiling. The strips were translucent so that you saw light all around you but couldn't see beyond the strips immediately in front of you. In fact, the strips were all over you, and the way forward involved making a swimming motion with your arms. As you did this, you would pick up static electricity from rubbing the plastic. As you would be swimming along, every now and then, the electricity would discharge sending a sizable spark forward to the person in front of you. They would jump, wince, and yip with the crack of a spark. You could feel the zaps.

The yellow footprints led us through a maze of twists and turns so that we lost our sense of direction. From every direction in the room, we heard Ows and Oos and saw flashes of sparks being discharged. The sparks tingled and made you squeamish trying to avoid the next one. The only way to avoid collecting electrons was to stop. But you had to go on, and to go on you had to brush up against more strips. At first, it was fun. Then it became oppressive. After a while, it seemed endless. The whole journey lasted about twenty minutes, but we had no idea how long we would be in there. My idea of <u>art</u> at the time didn't include being lost on a swim through plastic strips while being zapped with electricity. I had to recalibrate my notion of "art."

Least-Worst Cook, Cooks

We lived in an apartment. My wife worked full time. I worked part-time and was a full-time graduate student. We would take turns cooking dinner. Neither of us was particularly hot on the idea of cooking dinner. Our incentives for cooking diverged. I liked to eat. I looked forward to dinner. I didn't snack. I enjoyed good food. She liked to eat sometimes. She could take a full dinner or leave it. She snacked. Good food was optional.

Over time, the dinners became simpler and simpler. They became more basic. The frills and flourishes were gone. We were down to a starch, a veggie, and meat. Then the disaster struck. She made spaghetti but overcooked it. It was awfully gummy. It had Ragu sauce on it straight out of the jar. There was no Parmesan cheese. It was hard to get down. She had trouble with it too.

I pulled off a better but mediocre meal the next night. She followed it with hamburgers that floated in grease — the old heartburn special. This was hardly edible. She proclaimed that she was not as good a cook as I was. Maybe I should do the cooking since I was fussier. This was said in all disingenuousness.

The next night I over boiled a cottage ham; it was dry as shoe leather. The potatoes disintegrated in the pot and the cabbage was mush. She ate it and said, "Not bad!" I was losing the competition. The next night, she broiled a steak. We sat talking about the day as the steak cooked.

Smoke began pouring out of the kitchen. I said, "My god, aren't you going to rescue it?" She took her time walking to the kitchen. The steak was a char. There was no choice but to throw it down the incinerator chute. No dinner! At that point, I knew I had lost. I cared if I ate at all. She could live on some snacks.

The Conductor

A great piano teacher at the Cleveland Institute of Music gave a recital of Bach's Well Tempered Clavier. The work consisted of twenty-four preludes and fugues. Arthur Loesser played the pieces from memory. The audience overflowed the auditorium. The remaining people were seated on the stage right behind Loesser. My friend Joe and I had some of these prime seats. Joe was an aspiring music student and composer.

As Loesser played, I noticed a woman in the front row of the audience waving her arms. She had a large copy of the score. It was so big that it intruded on the space of those sitting next to her. As she followed the score and turned the big pages, she would conduct Loesser. Of course, Loesser noticed none of this. He was deeply engrossed in playing. Her waving, however, was a terrible distraction to those sitting around her.

About half way through the pieces, Loesser began playing quite a few measures of another prelude and then stopped dead in his tracks. He said to the audience that he started the wrong one. He apologized for taking one of them out of sequence. He then began playing the right one. Meanwhile, the woman was red in the face. She had been following the score and waving her arms to the wrong piece! So much for affectation!

The Free Christmas Tree

We moved to our apartment in Cleveland Heights and were pretty well established. My wife had grown up in relative poverty and was very sensitive about money. If she had an impulse to buy something, she didn't want to be denied. I was the brake on these impulses but I didn't succeed in curbing many of them, at least, not without much rancor. Every week she made sure she spent all of her paycheck. I was the saver. I saved part of my fellowship as well as part of earnings from a parttime job. My savings didn't amount to much.

Christmas Eve was upon us. We had boxes of tree decorations from my parents when they downsized and moved to an apartment. We had no tree. I proposed that we buy a tree from a nearby Catholic Church's annual tree sale. We got there about ten thirty at night, and the lot was empty. The sale signs were gone. I guessed that they sold all of their trees and went home. Wait, wait! There was a short odd-shaped tree with a crooked trunk. It had big holes in it with areas of missing needles. It was sitting right there in plain view. It looked like it had been through the mill. It was humble, but it was a tree.

The poor little tree was abandoned, left behind, no one wanted it. The church volunteers didn't even take the time to throw it away. Maybe they left it for anyone that would take it. It was right there in the middle of the lot, not thrown to the side or in a dumpster. I said, "There's nowhere else that we can find a tree on Christmas Eve. Let's give that tree a home." She said, "No, you can't take it. That would be stealing. You don't know that they want someone to take it." I replied, "But it's abandoned." She said, "You have to leave money for it." I said, "Fine, but there's no place to leave money. There's no one around here. It's Christmas Eve. Everybody is home or at church." She said, "You would want a free tree. You don't want to pay for things."

She was calling me cheap. She pushed my "cheap button." I said, "I can't just leave the money in the middle of the parking lot." As if I was riding around looking for a free tree. I wanted to pay for it. We ended up taking the little guy home and made it special with all of our decorations.

Switchboard Problems

During a hot summer of inner-city riots, I worked the switchboard of a major university in the inner city. It was a summer job, and they scheduled me on weekends. On weekends I worked there alone. The switchboard was located in an old hotel on the fringes of the campus. I quickly realized that everyone seeking contact with anyone at the university came through my board.

Some faculty were part of The Movement. They protested for civil rights and against the Viet Nam War. Some were involved in civil disobedience. Right wing people and groups had it in for these faculty. They called in with hostile tone asking for the faculty member. After there was no pickup, they harassed me by trying to pry private and emergency phone numbers from me. Some threatened me. They accused the university of communist sympathies. I tried to be polite even when they said they would get me.

The medical school accepted bodies donated to science. When a person died at home, funeral and transportation costs were saved because the university sent their vehicle to pick up the body. The university agreed to collect the cadavers in a timely manner. However, on weekends during the summer, many people were on vacation. Staffing was at a minimum. No one wanted to be bothered on their vacation or weekend. A wife would come to the phone and say, "He is not here." She would say it in a cautious half-hearted way. If I painted it as a real emergency, I would hear what sounded like much whispering. She would then say that he just walked through the door. Magic!

The family member with the dead body in the bed- room wanted it removed as soon as possible. Dying is often painful. The dead person often has a terrible look frozen on their face. The family member often doesn't like being in a room with the deceased. Here I was, a twenty-two-year-old graduate student trying to help solve such problems.

I was warned that the animals in the research labs were valuable. Some of them were part of experiments lasting many years. If the air conditioning in the lab failed, the animals could be dead in hours. On a blistering hot day, when the power went out, I raised a hue and a cry. The maintenance people jumped to it. Private contractors were notified. We saved the animals.

The Worry About Big Missiles

I got some relief from my life-long worry about nuclear war. I was working a part-time job reshelving books at a CWRU library. On my lunch breaks, I read newspapers. One day out of the blue, the national papers had stories, many on the front page, about the Soviet military threat.

There were pictures of Russian tanks. They were bigger than our tanks. They had more tanks than we had. There was a graphic comparing Russian ICBM's with our ICBM's. The Russian missiles were enormous, two or three times the size of ours. Such news stories were just the sort of thing that made me fearful growing up. This time, I became suspicious. If this threat was so great, why did it just arise as news? The big tanks and missiles didn't just happen one day.

I thought about it. Our defense budget was a multiple of the Soviet's. If our industrial base can build anything big, it was tanks. Can we build bigger missiles than the Russians? Of course, we can. We already had during the space race. What was going on here? I discovered that this was the time of year when the defense budget went before Congress. The Pentagon held press briefings that ginned up the Russian threat to sell the defense budget to the public. The reporters wrote articles based on what Pentagon officials had told them.

Who were the news stories directed toward? Was it the politicians? Not really. They knew the score. They had been in committees discussing the Defense Bill for months. Was it the reporters? Not really. They were keeping track of Russian capabilities all along. I concluded that the threats were directed at the public. The aim was to scare us so that we would not object to the magnitude of the defense bill.

At that moment, I became more cynical. I didn't like becoming more cynical. As you can tell from this book, I didn't need more cynicism. The major news outlets were in league with the defense department. In effect, they were inducing fear in the public to ramp up defense spending.

The upside of my realization was that there was no "new" need to fear the Soviets. They weren't trying to scare us. Our government was trying to scare us. The threats were for domestic political manipulation.

I slept more soundly that night. On that score, I kept sleeping soundly. We never did build bigger tanks, or more of them, or enormous missiles to match the Soviets.

Raw Political Art

My friend Joe Sekon, aspired to become a composer. He is the same Joe I mentioned attended Cleveland Orchestra half-concerts and the Arthur Loesser recital (above). After majoring in music as an undergraduate, he attended graduate school at the University of Illinois Champagne/Urbana. One of his professors, Salvatore Martirano, put together a theater piece and went on the road with it. Joe and Salvatore were to do a presentation at nearby Oberlin College. Joe invited my wife and me to experience the piece.

This was the late sixties when The Movement against the Viet Nam War was in full bloom. Campus protests were abundant, and Oberlin was a center for anti-war activity. Salvatore's piece was about political authorities committing physical violence against the public. His piece was called, "L'sGA" short for Lincoln's Gettysburg Address. It was for gas-masked politico, helium bomb, two channel tape, three films, and the dead rising from their graves.

Joe told us that news organizations in New York City like Time Inc. would sell film footage from their stockpile. When they would shoot a news story, they would use only a small percentage of the 16mm film they shot. The rest they would sell for twelve cents a foot. Salvatore went to their stockpile and bought film that was edited into the movies for L'sGA. A lot of the footage not used by the news organizations was the most violent and bloody stuff.

Salvatore picked out some horrible images. Japanese student riots where the students battled police with batons. Confrontations between police and union members on picket lines. His most nauseating images were of actual NAZI officers during World War II riding toy tanks over nude women lying flat on a big battlefield map. Salvatore had three of these sorts of composite images going on three adjacent screens at the same time.

Joe mentioned that Japanese arts authorities hired Salvatore to present the piece in Tokyo. They asked him what he needed. This was a dangerous thing to ask an artist. Apparently, cost was not a factor. Salvatore had them build three giant screens. It must have been incredible.

The gas-masked politico recited the Gettysburg Address. When he got to some phrases, he spoke with a German accent, "There is one great task remaining before us. There is one great task remaining before us!" The helium was slowly released into the mask so that the pitch of the politico's voice rose. The line, "of the people, by the people, and for the people," was changed to "up the people, try the people, fwock the people." The dead started rising from their graves going like zombies after the politico. By the end of the address, the politico was speaking in an emasculated, child's voice. The piece concluded with repetitions of "If it's sour, throw it out."

The theater was packed with students. There was very loud chatter and conversation before the piece. After the performance was over, there was dead silence. Everyone left the theater not saying a word. We felt numb too. If Salvatore wanted a conversation stopper, he found it. I took the polite message of the piece to be that political speech, no matter how celebrated, was used to mask political violence. Martirano brought home that message viscerally.

Afterwards, Joe, my wife, and I went to various houses to take in the weekend partying at Oberlin. One house stands out. There was an empty dining room with a plastic dry-cleaner bag hanging from the center of the ceiling. It was lighted so that the plastic dripped in a bowl below. People sat along the walls of the room breathing in the toxic fumes. Ultraviolet spotlights shined on the dripping bag giving it a bluish color. A strobe light went on and off periodically. As the flame melting the bag would go out, someone from the perimeter would get up and light it again. My goodness, what were those very intelligent students doing? We didn't stay there very long.

Salvatore recorded a LP record of the audio portion of L'sGA. He signed my copy. You can still buy a copy online.

Beer Refrigerator

I made beer. I made it eight gallons at a time. I collected quart ginger ale bottles. At the time, they were returned for a deposit. Any bottle returned for a deposit was used again. In order to be used again, it had to go through a very high temperature bottle washing process. In order to survive this process, it had to be made of quality glass, the kind of glass that could withstand the high pressure of fermented beer. Washing the bottles was the most labor-intensive part of making beer. Boiling them took forever. The alternative was to put a chlorine bleach solution in each bottle and then swish it around. The chlorine left a residual odor even after many rinses.

While a senior in college, a religion professor invited students to his home for a home brew party. I went with my friend John. The professor shared the recipe with anyone who wanted it. I decided to try it. I started out making a very basic beer. I graduated into beers that were a little smoother. I found a source for hops. I used good quality brewers' yeast. I bought a vat and a bottle capper. I also needed a second refrigerator to store the beer because the beer could not be left out; the bottles would explode. So, we had two refrigerators. One for food; one for beer.

The cost of producing the beer at the time was eleven cents a quart. It was an acquired taste, but everyone who drank enough of it came to like it more than regular beer. Regular beer was a malt soup that was injected with carbon dioxide. It tasted thin as dish water. Commercial beer was filtered to remove the yeast. It was dead. The FDA classified it as a beverage—- the same category as soda pop. Real beer was food. It was rich in B vitamins; the yeast remained as a nutrient.

Anyway, we invited people over for parties. They drank much beer. They returned with their friends. The rest was history. We had an endless string of parties. I was making beer every week. A number of our drinking buddies began making beer of their own. This was during the time of the counter culture, Woodstock, The Whole Earth Catalog, self-reliance, independence, a new age.

I was fermenting a new batch of beer when I noticed a

several-inch-wide green island growing on the top of my vat. "What in the world is that?" I exclaimed. I called the Poison Control Center. The lady on the line did not have the foggiest idea whether my green island was benign or a killer. She humored me, but I could tell that she wanted to move on to things that she knew something about. I scraped off the thick green floater. I bottled the beer. For the next round of parties, I had a good conversation starter.

After my wife and I divorced, not for beer related reasons, I lived with a friend Joe B. I brought along a dozen bottles of beer. I put them in heavy paper shopping bags. I put the bags in the closet. One July night I had company, and I heard this "ping" "ping" sound. It took a moment for it to dawn on me what that sound was. I ran to the closet. The beer bottles were bursting. The shattering glass of one shattered the glass of another. The paper bags had several inches of beer in them. I grabbed the handles and ran down the hall to the bathroom with paper bags full of beer! The bottom of one bag gave way before I reached the bathtub. There was beer and broken glass all over the hall.

Late Comers

The old apartment buildings, built in the 1930's, had apartments that were designed in a plan of a long hall with rooms off of it. The kitchen was in the back, living room in front and everything else in the middle. The hall was like a spine with the head, the living room, the stomach the kitchen and the other rooms arranged like a liver, kidney and so on. Well, that stretches the metaphor a bit too far, but you know what I mean. Anyway, the back door led onto an iron back porch with iron stairs going from floor to floor

We gave parties and freely invited people. If we invited 30 people, 20 would show up. Some with ego problems would often come late. The most important person was the last to arrive. Heavens if he or she should serve as the receiving line for someone else. "We are important — an audience is required for our entrance. There are so many pressing social demands made on us. We could barely tear ourselves away." If the party was raucous, the late-comers were hardly noticed. If the party was quiet, they made their grand entrance.

Well, most everyone resented the important few, and during one party we were talking about it and a brilliant flash came to me. We'll throw another party and invite some of the self-important people we know. We'll tell them that the party starts at seven o'clock sharp. At about eight, we will post a lookout and when one is on the way up the stairs, everyone but me will go out the back door and down the fire escape. When the grand entrance begins, only I will be there to greet them. Then, everyone else will start arriving in 2's and 3's every few minutes by the front door, not letting on that their arrival was pre-planned. Each of us will get a good look at the crimped expression of the self-important so and so's.

We tried the tactic on two royally self-important friends, but not all of us could keep a straight face. After they let on that they knew something was fishy, we sent them down the metal stairs to arrive fashionably late for the next latecomer. I must say that our targets were peeved!

Post Party Rush Hour

We sat on the floor looking at thick candles as the birds began to sing; it was time for the party to end with breakfast at Joe B's. We were surprised to see the long single file line of cars running in the predawn minutes. Silence, birds singing, and the single file running of the pre-rush hour cars. We were somewhere within the progression of moods that spilled over from the party. At this stage, we were feeling mellow easily tripping into laughter in spite of much fatigue. But strawberries, crepes, and whipped cream at Joe's was attractive enough to cause us to migrate.

As we walked on the sidewalk a few feet from the single file of predawn rush hour cars, we began expressing views to the effect that "those people are crazy." Joan said that we were inevitably going to end up doing the same thing. Tony replied that the only thing inevitable was that "those people" will continue doing what they were in the habit of doing. The corker was that in an instant, we had the same idea that,

"Maybe these people were happy doing what they were doing. Our harsh assessment was beside the point of their personal experience." So, we spontaneously personalized it.

We kept walking but turned so that we could see the traffic moving in the direction we were walking. We looked into those faces for signs or even a glint of happiness. What we saw were gray, lifeless, catatonic faces grimly applied to the task at hand. They seemed to be removed from themselves. They expressed emotion only indirectly through the running of their car engines. Contact with these expressions was quite unexpected. It did not fit our feelings of the moment. So, we began to smile at them and wave to them and salute them and bow to them, and laugh and laugh and laugh. The mockery of course brought out anger, hostility and more intense driving.

I did not like the thought of upsetting people so that they were a knot of misplaced aggression. We rationalized our foolishness by agreeing that we at least brought out some human feeling — something that was genuine and tied to the moment. But better that they feel intense resentment and hatred than nothing? The numbing dawn was breaking where the soft grays of the night turned over to intense sunlight. Our eyes were frozen in the strain that only daybreak can cause. Our tone sobered up a bit, and after that crepes with strawberries, a round on the throne, and "ho hum" a nap.

Cutting Bottles

The counter culture was in full bloom. Self-reliance, a return to the land, communal activities, and a simplified life were the lure for suburbanite kids. The Whole Earth Catalog presented the tools for making alternative living possible. I rejected materialism. In my apartment, I had only what I needed. My Peugeot 10 speed. Minimal place settings of dishes. German stereo components. My book and record collection. My violin. My paintings.

The Whole Earth Catalog had a nice description of a bottle cutter. It enabled you to take any bottle and cut the top off of it. After this, you sanded the edge smooth or melted the edge with a torch. You could make an ashtray out of the bottom of a quart bottle. You could make drinking glasses out of beer bottles. You could take pop bottles with Dr. Pepper or Hires Root Beer painted on their sides and turn them into soda glasses. Wine bottles have that intriguing indentation at their bottoms. Cut off the top and you have an interesting, odd-sized vase.

After getting good at cutting bottles, and it didn't take long, I set out to get a dozen empty wine bottles. We thought that the best place would be a restaurant. They served up many cases of wine in an evening. It was Sunday and most restaurants were closed. We hunted behind them for the empties. No empties were there. We thought that the trash was already collected. Our search took us many miles from Cleveland into a Ritzy suburb where the Hunt Club crowd lived. I decided to ask for empty bottles. A maitre d' told us that all wine bottles needed to be returned to their cases for inventory! The state regulated the wine business. I guess it was trying to prevent bottles from leaving restaurants.

Throwing Dishes

I had gotten a job teaching philosophy part-time at Cuyahoga Community College. As an employee, I was entitled to one free course. I decided to take ceramics. My ulterior motive was to make a range of house hold items for my use. I made a couple of ash trays. I made tea pots. I built them from slabs. Slab building allowed for more creativity than using a potter's wheel. You worked the clay like dough and then cut it into sheets. You form the sheets into objects such as tea pots. I made cups too. One of my cups had a lip like a human lip. When you drank from it, your lips lipped the lip. Another cup had the handle built into the body of the cup. This cut down on the amount of liquid that the cup could hold. Because of shrinkage in the firing process, my cups came out too small to be practical. They were decorative.

Our teacher encouraged us well enough. He said that any pot that did not work out could serve as a cactus planter. One way that pots did not work out was that its walls were too thick. The pot would be heavy and bulky. Not much craft there. Where is the cactus? My aim in using the potter's wheel was to throw a set of dishes. I made ten of them. They had two-tone glaze: tan with large white swirls. The ceramics served a good purpose. I used them for many years. I gave many of them away as gifts. Since I had enough pieces, I did not take ceramics again.

Chapter XI

Enterprising Education

It was hard to live on a part-time college teacher's pay. Administrators always said that it was not exploitation, that is, the low pay. They said that you were not expected to live on it. It was supposed to be extra money on top of your day job. But many courses were offered during the day at the same low rate. They still did not expect you to live on it. No full-time positions were currently open in my field. If no full-time job was available, I would be enterprising. I would offer my own philosophy courses.

I ran an ad in the Cleveland Plain Dealer. An editor called me, thinking that I was some charlatan trying to take advantage of the public. He was satisfied that I was legitimate when I informed him about my college degrees. My friends, though, thought that I was unrealistic. I told them that we can't know about the demand for my services unless we find out through spreading the word. Maybe there is a vast untapped market that would beat its path to my apartment door.

The first call I got was from a woman who expressed great interest in coming to the lectures. In a few minutes, I got another call from someone who claimed to be her brother. He threatened me after accusing me of trying to take advantage of his sister. I gathered that his sister, for whatever reason, required looking after and was not in a position to make her own choices. I assured him that I did not know his sister and did not want to take advantage of her.

Several people said that they would come to the lecture and pay the nominal fee. I think that it was five in all. I quickly enlisted several friends to fill out the audience. This was just in case only one or two people came. It would appear that there was face-saving interest in my lectures. I made some punch. I bought some cookies. Set up some chairs. Borrowed a chalk- board. I received my friends and waited for the class to arrive. Only two people showed up. One was a retired gentleman. One was a new mother. Neither expressed much interest in philosophy. I tried to tie them into the discussion. My friends and I carried the day. While I saved face, the battle was lost. There was no point to promoting private college level instruction.

Washing Dishes

After the divorce, I was more interested in simplifying my life by eliminating material things. I now had the power to stem the flow of stuff into my living space. My motto was, "Things of the spirit are the things that count." Books, records, musical instruments, and tools are of the spirit. They involve self-application, personal development, or aid in problem-solving. The rest is mostly utilitarian or ornamental at best. My aims were to avoid hoarding, not falling prey to advertisers, and actively applying my sense of value. I can honestly say that I never consciously bought a product because of an advertisement.

At worst, stuff required fixing, cleaning, storage, replacement, and so on. There was also the mere physical presence of objects that crowded life. You had to walk around them, pick them up, and keep track of them. Then there was the preoccupation with acquiring more, the shopping trips, the planning. You could slip into your whole life being in servitude to physical stuff. My mother called a lot of it, "dust collectors." Upon dying, all of my possessions would most likely end up in a landfill anyway. So, I should live with the things of the spirit. They would help me stay alive.

To a greater degree, I was now master of my fate, captain of my ship. Well, all of that sounds too dramatic. So, let's bring the discussion down to the practical. How should I handle dishes and silverware? I could make those things into things of the spirit by making my own. I already (above) told tales of making dishes in ceramics class and cutting bottles for glasses and glassware. My not very original idea was that a utilitarian object can be beautiful and express my developed sensibilities. My present problem was how much of that stuff to make or acquire. Too many ceramics classes and the dust collectors would pile up. Also, there was the problem of keeping dishes and silverware clean. The quantity and cleaning questions figured into the spirit question.

Only rarely did I enjoy washing dishes. So, did I need more dishes or less? If I had more dishes, I could let them pile up until I was in the mood to wash them. If the mood didn't strike me, I would run out of clean dishes and silverware and the sink would be overloaded.

An artist friend of my ex-wife, Ken Nevadomi, was rumored to let the dirty dishes pile up. He would then put them in the bath tub, put in soap, and run the water. I suppose that he had in mind something like a factory. Why mess around with a few dishes here or there. Do them on an industrial scale.

So, a solution to the dish-problem was to get more of them. If you have enough of them, you might not have to wash dishes for a month. That did not appeal to my sense of simplicity. I would run into the problem of stuff getting in my way with piles of dirty dishes everywhere. The thought of how dreadful it would be to live in such clutter would affect my mental health. Depression would set in and my other things of the spirit would be compromised.

Besides, it would feel better to have a clean kitchen and sink. Do dishes after every meal? The thought of regimentation was not appealing. If I was tired and ready to relax, I would let the dirty dishes slide for a while. I had been there before.

I decided to have two place settings—— two dinner plates, two salad bowls, two sets of silverware, and four pots for cooking. I chose two settings because at some point I would have a guest for dinner, and I didn't want to be short a plate. After dinner I would be motivated to wash them. I quickly formed the habit of doing the dishes while my coffee water was boiling. The small number of dishes assured I would get them done in a few moments. The dread would not set in.

A Bed for a Man

I also worked part-time teaching philosophy for Cleveland State University in the inner city. A student suggested that I move into an old neighborhood close to the university. He called it "new town." Many of his friends, counter culture all, were taking advantage of the neat old houses and low rent. I saw a sign advertising a house for rent. A middle aged, excited lady answered the door. She appeared to be the sort of person who was nearly hysterical most of the time. Her son of about seven years old appeared to be autistic. He was constantly animated, throwing things or running around. He had pointy ears. The owner was six feet something, gaunt, thin, and slow of speech.

Some friends helped me move in. I had been sleeping on a cot borrowed from a friend, but I had to give it back. When I was moving in, the landlord asked where my bed was. I said that I had none. He then said that there was a spare bed in the tenant house behind his. He rented it to a six foot eight, three-hundred- pound hippie poet who stammered. He knocked on his door. With repeated knocks, finally, the enormous guy answered. The landlord said that he wanted the spare bed. The enormous guy resisted letting us in.

The tenant house was in shambles. You could hardly move through it. We recovered the bed. When we separated the mattress from the box spring, there was this peeling sound. There was a large patch of dried vomit in the center. Apparently, someone puked on the mattress and instead of cleaning it up, flipped it. There it dried. The landlord pretended not to see the vomit. He called in his wife. "Connie, clean this up. We can't have this man sleeping on a mattress like this. Someone might have urinated in it."

I loaded the mattress with every sheet and blanket I had to isolate myself from making contact with it and went to sleep.

The Rug

I moved in the second story of the house with the landlord below me. The biting November winds were kicking up and the nights were quite cold. The apartment was heated by a gas burner. The room got progressively colder as I moved in concentric rings away from the burner. The burner had no fan. The burner had no pilot light; every time, I had to light it with a match.

On my first night there, I tried everything I knew to light the gas burner. I failed. I concluded that since the gas did not hiss when I opened the valve, the pressure must be very low. The landlord was not home, so I got out some extra blankets and toughed out the night.

The next day I caught the landlord going out, and I told him about the trouble I had with the heater. He took me to the basement and showed me how the gas company had come out and shut off and sealed my gas meter. I told him that I owed the gas company no money; I was a new customer. He told me that they made a mistake in confusing his meter with mine. He could not pay his bill, so they came out to shut off his meter but instead shut off mine by mistake. He told me that they did this when only his wife was home and she did not know which meter was which. From this incident I concluded that my landlord was living on the edge of insolvency and he would use trickery to preserve comforts for himself and his family.

The life pattern of people in poverty can't be imagined by those living a middle-class life. The necessities of life consume all of a person's waking hours. There is a logic dictated by necessity. My landlord was a house painter with jobs few and far between. The woodwork and floor in my living room were painted with brown paint. You knew it wasn't stain or varnish because it looked like brown paint. It looked o.k. as what you would do in an old house if you did not want to strip the wood.

My living room floor had a fake American Indian rug that did not look too fake, at least to me. It was very worn which made it look less fake. One day when I was vacuuming it and around it on the brown paint, a corner was lifted by the vacuum cleaner and a bit of natural wood appeared. I lifted the rug and found that the center of the floor was unpainted. The wood was old, dusty, and gray. The brown paint extended a few inches underneath the border of the rug.

Apparently, my landlord measured and centered the rug and then painted a frame for it on the floor. Why wouldn't he just paint the whole floor? He achieved the desired effect using half the paint and paint costs money. The logic of poverty took over. Many people in the neighborhood taped newspaper over their windows. They did not have money for curtains. Why not leave the windows bare? I was told that when you go to work someone may look in, break in, and steal your TV.

The Shower in Purgatory

My rental unit was half downstairs and half upstairs. The kitchen was down and the living space was up. The trouble was that the kitchen was not heated. As the winter approached, I spent less and less time in the kitchen. Between the two spaces, about six steps up from the kitchen was a landing. Off the landing was the shower. The heat from the living space would descend part way down the stairs but not quite to the shower. It was bloody cold in the shower. I would run down the stairs into the shower. I had goose bumps all over. I would hate to pull back the shower curtain. When I did a burst of frigid air would hit me, and I would run upstairs to dry off.

The Produce Gourmet

For the time being, I decided to try to live in respectable poverty. In America, this was challenging. I decided to be as self-sufficient as possible. I started to roll my own cigarettes. I bought a little device that would make the cigarettes come out sort of round. I had my can of Bugle tobacco. As I smoked these full-strength unfiltered cigarettes, my nicotine addiction worsened. Finally, I would be having dreams about smoking a cigarette. It would wake me up in the middle of the night. I would smoke up and go back to bed. I went back to commercial cigarettes.

In the area of town with major museums and Case Western University, there was a food coop. I worked as a buyer. Our buying team would be at the food terminals at five AM as the trucks of produce were being unloaded. Many of the vendors personally knew the grocers that bought from them. The grocers did not like the food coop. It cut into their business. For my work as a buyer, I got a very low price on a weekly bag of fruits and vegetables. Meat was expensive. I decided to eat mostly rice, soy beans, and cheese for my protein. It was a healthy diet. Lots of vegetables and fruits along with a rice or bean dish.

The first night I tried to make a soy meat loaf. It was a fake meat loaf. It was supposed to look like one. It was supposed to simulate one. I knew it wouldn't taste like one. The trouble with the recipe was that it took a long time to prepare. I first had to boil the beans. My kitchen was on the first floor, and it was unheated. I went upstairs to warmth.

Well, the water boiled away, and the beans began to burn. I smelled them. I ran down stairs. I had to sort through the beans one by one in order to salvage the edible ones. My meat loaf was puny. It did not taste good. Adding more spices didn't help. I ate mostly celery and spinach for dinner. I never did learn how to work with and enjoy soy beans.

Some vendors at the food terminal sold household products like paper and soap. I thought that I would save money by buying in bulk. I bought a carton of toilet paper. I bought twenty-four cans of cleanser. The toilet paper lasted more than six months. The cleanser lasted several years. Every time I moved to another rental unit, I had to lug the carton of cleanser cans. It was also irritating that the price of cleanser did not go up much in those years. I could have gotten as good a deal buying the cans as I needed them from the supermarket.

Home Is Where The Feud Is

An old buddy of the landlord named Buck was visiting the house. Buck was a recovering alcoholic from southern Ohio who needed a place to crash. Buck was a sweet guy who told a good story in a gravelly voice—sort of like Robert Duvall in <u>Tender Mercies</u>. The landlord had a low opinion of him; he said Buck was weak and a mooch.

The landlord had gotten me that classic bed. I didn't have a refrigerator. He found a used one and asked me to help him and Buck pick it up. We were on our way to pick it up. I mentioned to Buck that I had seen some charred boards inside my back door in the mud room. Buck said nonchalantly, "Oh, the kids in the back firebombed the house." I didn't know about the kids in the back. My only exit was that back door.

The landlord's wife, who I described as unusually excitable, got into an argument with two teenage kids who lived behind her property. One kid punched her. When the landlord came home, he went there and beat the kid up. That's when, the next night, the house was firebombed. This happened before I moved in, but the kids still had it in for the landlord.

One night, Buck knocked on my door and said the landlord wanted to ask me a question. The landlord had a barely-functioning old truck. It was parked on the street. The kids had just broken out all of its windows. The landlord asked me what to do. I said that he should call the cops. I think he thought we all should go over there and even the score.

That night I had visions of another firebombing. I bought a fire extinguisher. A few days later I was coming home around 1 AM when I heard, "Hey, you!" I turned and there up the street was a guy with a shot gun. For some reason, I was not alarmed. I don't know why I wasn't alarmed. Maybe it was because he was not aiming it at me. I don't know.

As he walked under a street light, I recognized him as one of my students at the community college. There was a trucking company a block over with a number of loaded simi trailers. He was the night guard. But walking in the middle of the street with a shotgun?

It was still winter and I thought that once the hot weather comes, the people in the neighborhood would be more easily agitated. Shakespeare does a good job of integrating hot weather with helping set the mood for the fights in Romeo and Juliet. I thought I should move out before something major happens. When the Spring thaw came, I moved out of "New Town" back into Cleveland Heights.

Lost Knowledge

I went to a book sale at a library in one of Cleveland's wealthy suburbs close to my new digs. I found a copy of Alexander Solzhenitsyn's The Gulag Archipelago. I thought that the library must be mistaken. They should have kept that book. What were they doing selling it? I checked their card catalog. There were no copies of the book left in their library system. It was gone! I asked a librarian why they eliminated it. She said that if a book didn't circulate, then it was removed from the shelves.

I realized, with a very empty feeling, that great books of every sort wouldn't make that cut. Kant, Milton, Newton, Tolstoy, Einstein wouldn't show up on very many shelves. If I thought they should keep books like those, would I have to keep checking the books out so that they would remain available to the public?

Kidding aside, then current reality was that even if a book about Einstein was on a shelf, Einstein wasn't. What public library had any books or collections of papers by him? What about Euclid's Elements? What about Plato's dialogs?

I believed that what's not in a library was probably more important than what was in it. To a young person of my time, the understanding of reality outside of immediate experience was, in important ways, limited to what was there on the shelves.

I knew that some important knowledge was in great and difficult books. Retrieving that knowledge was arduous and capable of only a very few. Aristotle's ethical theory, for example, provided answers to problems of conduct beyond the point reached by most current psychologists. The course of our civilization would have been free from some intractable problems if Aristotle were widely understood all along. Why this didn't happen, however, goes well beyond the practices of libraries.

If as a society we recognized that the human heritage of achievement contained knowledge desperately needed today, great books and a large array of others would remain on library shelves. But the public was not taught to go to books to solve problems. Nonetheless, I thought that we needed to start somewhere. I advocated that great books should be there for the aspiring public. They should be there to represent human achievement. They could serve as a beacon for the young.

You may regard this view as eccentric. I came to it through hard experience as a teacher. Limiting opportunity stifles growth. Even if the public didn't look for a book on a certain topic, that doesn't show they don't <u>need</u> the book. In fact, you could argue that many answers to current problems that really bother people are already in some book or another.

I thought of two questions to those who controlled accessibility to books. The first is the old saw, "Does every generation need to reinvent the wheel?" The second is loaded. "Who is wise enough to know which books should be excluded from a collection?" Statistics on circulation as a basis for pulling books was mindless.

So, local libraries should not just cater to the tastes of the surrounding public. Doing that just echoes the average education of the public. It assures gray democracy.

The Harpsichord

I loved music. I wanted to play music. I was a drummer in high school. I took violin lessons in college. I got A's in my violin courses. Even so, I could not hear well enough to carry a steady pitch. I took up the violin because there was so much great music written for it. There were certain pieces that I wanted to play. So, I gave private violin lessons one more try. After work with a disappointing teacher, I decided that I would not play an instrument that required me to create pitches. I wanted to play a machine that was already tuned.

The piano is a glorious instrument. But I didn't want to play the piano. The piano music that interested me most was enormously difficult to play well. I loved much of the music written for the piano's predecessor — the harpsichord. The only problem was that in Cleveland at the time there weren't technicians who could tune or repair harpsichords. I didn't want to buy an expensive instrument from a craftsman and then not be able to tune it. In being expensive, I would also be squeamish about working on it for fear that I might leave it in worse condition.

After reading some books on harpsichords, I decided to build my own. The books gave a sure-fire technique for tuning the instrument. I learned that a tuner did not have to have perfect pitch. After building the instrument, I would not be afraid of working on it. I would have mastered all of the techniques needed to keep the instrument playing. I ordered my harpsichord kit.

One day at my doorstep, I found two large boxes. They contained about one hundred and thirty pieces of wood. The instruction manual was about forty pages long on typed single-spaced pages. The first task was to take a ruler and measure each piece of wood. The measurement was supposed to match a parts list. Piece by piece you would check off the items on the list. This was in order to help the builder gain familiarity with the parts, most of which had special names like belly rail stiffner, cheek, and nut.

I worked on the instrument on and off for about two years. About one third of the time was in building the box. Another third was in finishing and painting it. The last third was in installing the musical parts. The result was much better than I expected. It sounded wonderful. It looked sharp. I was on my way to playing interesting music that moved my heart.

Over the Counter Culture

For a time, I lived in the alternate lifestyle part of a suburb. The Coventry area was home to artists, academics, musicians, college students, and many professional people. There also were alternate lifestyle sorts who did a lot of drugs and experimented with various sorts of non-conventional sexual orientations and lifestyles. The outside culture's label for many of them was "Hippie." Of course, there were genuine dyed in the wool hippies. But then, there were the believers in natural foods. There were the experimenters with artificial drugs. There were the commune types. There were the devotees of far Eastern religion.

Coventry Road contained shops to cater to these groups. There were clothing stories, a drug paraphernalia shop, a bookstore, a leather store, candle store and so on. People would get together on the street especially at night. The weekends were another story. Suburbanites from all over would come to Coventry to hang out. Many of them bought expensive hippie clothing and carried hippie accessories. Locals called them "The Saturday Hippies." They dressed up like hippies, and then went down to Coventry to make the scene.

Their hippie costumes stood out like sore thumbs. New fashionable clothes? Clothes made to look tattered and worn but which looked off the rack? I didn't despise them their lark. Many were very young kids searching for an identity. Project this trend nationally and you have what Madison Avenue did to The Movement. Cash in on the hippie trend. Everyone can look like a hippie! You can buy the appearance of the identity. What Madison Avenue called, "The Counter Culture," I called, "The Over the Counter Culture." The counter culture label was just one more advertising scheme.

The Witch in Biology Lab

In the 1970's teachers made an effort to respect the diversity of the student population. At the time, diverse cultural groups were expecting to be acknowledged. A person's religion should not make him or her an outcast or an object of derision. A white-haired woman appeared in a biology class at Cuyahoga Community College. She claimed that she was a witch. Witch doctrine placed her within a pagan or maybe nature-worshipping religion. The primary animal to be dissected that term was a cat! The witch said that it was against her religion to dissect the cat. The teacher had someone else dissect the cat while the witch watched.

Cheap Cake

When getting a beer at a folk music bar, I met a woman who shared my desire for free living. The aim was to set out on a life path of continuing personal renewal. This was captured in the Bob Dylan line,

"He not busy being born is busy dying." Noel was good humored and a gentle soul. My artist friends and I decided to throw a birthday party for her.

I thought it would be fun to stretch a large canvas, about 5 by 6 feet, and have everyone participate in painting a painting for Noel at the party. Noted Cleveland artists Reed Thomason, Bob Raack, and Richard Smith were to do the major part of the painting. Several of us had to walk the canvas to the house. As we happily carried the canvas down the night-shadowed street, we anticipated the moxie of it all. We also knew that Noel would be surprised.

The painting went well in spite of half a dozen styles within it. Bob put in large human figures that defined the design. Richard worked on a color field. Reed painted a kettle of gold coins with a rainbow leading to it. I tried to work on transitions among these elements. The finished painting was Noel's birthday present.

We had to have a cake for Noel. Someone had the idea for a cheap cake. There was a bakery outlet nearby. People would call in orders for cakes. Sometimes people would not pick up their cakes. The bakery would be stuck with them. They would sell them for a very low price. Noel's cake had the scales of justice on it. Above the scales was the heading, "Congratulations Marcus." Apparently, Marcus was supposed to graduate from law school or pass the bar exam. I guess that Marcus didn't make it!

Chapter XII

Teaching Anew

I was in contention for two full-time jobs. Other teaching prospects looked good. This was because I was a wild card, education-wise. On my view, most of what passed for good teaching practice was woefully inadequate. I vowed not to visit on my students, the sins committed against me. My students would have learning opportunities that they could not even dream of. I was determined to avoid past mistakes. If I would make mistakes, they would be new, innovative, or original.

I was a severe critic of the status quo. Just how can someone spend twelve years in English classes and not be able to write a coherent sentence? How can someone after six years of history and social studies classes not know that there are two chambers of Congress? How can someone not know that the sun does not actually rise? Students had to be glazed over not to know basic information and skill.

The writer Paul Goodman pointed to a study done in Harlem in New York City. Up to fifth grade, black male students were on a par with their white counterparts. After fifth grade they saw a decrease in their IQ year by year. Someone with a 120 IQ in elementary school, ended up with an 85 IQ by the time they graduated from high school. School along with their personal lives was destroying their minds.

I had enthusiasm for breaking the mold. I wanted to try a large number of educational experiments. I wanted my students to have opportunities that few students had. This sort of direction struck a chord with college administrators. They wanted my innovative proposals to succeed. Students too liked my open approach to the classroom. On all sides, I had great support for getting a full-time job. I got my big chance.

Where's the knowledge?

I was hired as a full-time teacher in philosophy and the humanities at Cuyahoga Community College. For years I had been coming to grips with the commitment to become a teacher. I thought that most teachers didn't have much to teach. By this, I meant that much of what passed for curriculum was quite pointless for living life. There was much information and exercises of one kind or another but little that equipped the young to carry on with flourish, to live well personally and socially, and to develop their important talents.

From this critical angle, I could have talked myself out of becoming a teacher. What sort of material could stand up to such high standards? I needed something to teach that held up to scrutiny.

In choosing philosophy as a vocation, I had already decided that I didn't want to teach a variety of other subjects. Several potential majors fell away. The reason for this was that for the most part, the study of philosophy spoiled my idealism about many other fields.

Take history as an example. For starters a philosopher would ask, "What is history?" And then ask "What is good history?" Philosophers examine and evaluate the theories of most everything. Theories of history would present a point of view that would explain what history is, when it is well done, what it is for, and what could be gained through it. After digging into the philosophy of history, I became dissatisfied with what historians had accomplished and can accomplish.

There was nothing profound behind this conclusion. At the time, it was all about the basics. It started when I learned in a philosophy course that to have knowledge about something, you needed to meet the condition of having a justification. For a belief to be something you knew, it must be true as well as justification to support its truth.

The standard freshman English composition course had students learn research methods through writing a term paper. The support in the paper, or evidence for conclusions, had to be documented with sources in footnotes. So, arguing for a point of view required proof. Without proof, a conclusion may be true, but its truth has not been supported. I took a term paper without footnotes as presenting something less than knowledge. Perhaps, it would be only unsupported opinion.

At the time, when I browsed history books, I found few footnotes. Even the work of eminent historians rarely contained footnotes. Were they using less than adequate research methods? Had they only given their opinions. The opinions may be true, but the reader doesn't <u>know</u> they're true. I thought that many a historian's readership fell short of gaining knowledge from them. If many of the writers I was encountering were among the best historians of the time, where was the current historical <u>knowledge</u>? I asked myself the question as to where their material came from. Without proof, for all I knew, they could have been just making it all up.

The same thing happened with other subjects, including the sciences. Where in science textbooks were the footnotes? I checked my science textbooks. There were few to none. Minimally, I thought, the authors should inform the reader where to find the experiments that proved their main claims. Isn't science supposed to be based on evidence? Without evidence, the reader does not gain knowledge. My skepticism grew.

I also realized that there was no science called "Science." The sorts of questions I was asking were not addressed in science books. After an obligatory first chapter on scientific method, the textbooks I examined went on without following or referring to that method. I had to turn to the philosophy of science for answers. One topic in the philosophy of science was what a scientific theory is and why some theories are better than others.

As an undergraduate, I kept coming back to philosophical conceptions setting up inquiries into things. And with the sciences, even if a number of methods were somewhat different than in philosophy, the rationale for the methods was philosophical. Philosophy was unavoidable.

Bingo! Some Philosophy Worth Teaching

Being in philosophy did not solve my problem of finding something worth teaching. Philosophy has a very large domain. I believed that there was much in philosophy that wasn't worth the effort. And much worthwhile philosophical material could be approached badly through treating it as mere history supplemented with academic exercises. Furthermore, philosophy, like most fields, divided into a myriad of sub-specialties that were highly technical in nature. I wanted to teach college freshmen and sophomores with the focus <u>on them</u> and their lives. I used that view as primary in selecting what to teach.

Other criteria narrowed my view. From my college's point of view, my courses needed to be transferable to other institutions, fulfill degree requirements, set up further studies in a subject area, contrast with other disciplines, and inform students about the philosophical tradition. With all of that in mind, I thought about what particular material was best.

In the spirit of the 1960's, I needed to find reasons to teach this rather than that. I culled topics from the history of philosophy and from current discussions of philosophical problems that I thought were keys to advancing a person's thought. I chose the notion of "inquiry" as my main subject.

When you inquire, you try to find out about something. What do you need to know in order to do this? How can you become an independent thinker, meaning that you can inquire for yourself? Well, you need the background to evaluate results of your inquiry. You need criteria for deciding whether thinking is on the right track and how to judge the quality of its products.

A portion of this kind of material is in the branch of philosophy called logic. The field of logic advanced greatly in the 19th and 20th centuries. An important part of that advance was modern symbolic logic. It provided a basis for the computer revolution. I taught a logic course that featured some topics in symbolic logic. They were selected to fit a method for evaluating arguments. In the language of logic, in good arguments, conclusions can be correctly drawn from other statements called premises.

Fallacies Everywhere

Some topics in logic are essential for independent thinking. One topic of particular importance is the study of logical mistakes called fallacies. Many fallacies were categorized in ancient times by Aristotle. They were mistakes commonly made because there is a psychology behind them that is shared by all of us. It turns out that often what is psychologically persuasive is disconnected from what is concluded. Examples include attacking the speaker rather than their argument, hasty generalization, and appeal to fear.

To take these three examples of fallacies, we can imagine that the first thing propagandists of our time might do is call someone an abusive name. They might secondly take some exceptional case and treat it as the norm. Lastly, they might use threats to arouse fear. The name-calling, unwarranted generalization, and fear would have no bearing on the topic of the argument. In logic, we would say that they lack relevance for proving the conclusion.

It is sad that these mistakes are notoriously exploited for political gain. The internet and its absence of standards opened widespread abuse of reasoning to trick an uninformed public. Even the traditional media, whether it be liberal, conservative, or radical, don't "call out" logical errors. They act as if there were no such standards. Their behavior indicates, to me at least, that they as well as the two major political parties want to be able to manipulate the public to their ends.

The political parties continue to pound a drum for more donations to their organizations. This raises the question, "What is all that money being used for?" The usual answer is, "Political advertising." Are political ads used to make a case for a point of view? Usually not. Their aim is to bombard the public with manipulative appeals. Their aim is to persuade the public of what has not been proven.

Critical Thinking

What is beyond manipulation? The simple answer is making a case through defensible reasoning. Enter the study and application of logic. Almost universally, logic is not taught in primary and secondary school. I have argued that this should change. When young people learn to read, write, and speak, they should learn to reason and draw correct inferences. There is much missing from traditional language studies. One topic that is utterly missing is any conception of truth. Logic can't be applied to language without an understanding of what truth is.

Students from throughout my teaching career probably would roll their eyes when encountering the dumbing-down of discourse in the media and the endless resort to manipulation. The sad reality is that these tactics are just like what Aristotle encountered in 350 BC. Why hasn't our civilization learned to use good logic? That's another story.

In the 1980's, my approach to curriculum caught on when the critical thinking movement was born. Of course, I am not claiming credit for any role in bringing about the movement. It was just happenstance that my sort of curriculum was timely.

As with most innovations in education, however, critical thinking became a fad. Practically every educator at my institution and beyond claimed to be teaching critical thinking. What most of them did, however, was a dressed-up version of critical work in their field. Most didn't know how to teach logic. That's in part because most hadn't studied it.

My First Bribe

Legend has it that many students get by with bribes. It starts with apples in elementary school. It ends with all sorts of incentives in graduate school. When I started my job as a philosophy teacher. I waited to be corrupted. Bring on the goodies. At first, I thought that baked goods were going to come my way. None did. Then around exam time, I thought someone might regress into the apple inducement. None did. Sports tickets? None. Money? No student would be that crass. I was getting desperate. Being a college teacher was not what it was cracked up to be.

In my second semester Introduction to Philosophy course, lightning struck. The day before the final exam, a student stayed after class and told me about how he belonged to a fish and game club. He went fishing. He had an extra trout that he thought I should have! Here it was. My first bribe. A trout! Sure enough, before the final exam here he came with a newspaper bundle. He told me a little about broiling it and lemon butter and then sat down. After the exam, I told him that the trout was not going to affect his grade. He could take it back if he so chose. He wanted me to have it anyway. Great student! Very good trout!

Starting the Lawn Mower

Pam and I were on her ancestral farm in Michigan. We stayed in a tenant farmer house. The tenant farmers were long gone. The land was rented out for large-scale industrialized farming. In order not to be a complete mooch, I agreed to mow some of the grass. Almost all of the grass needed mowing. It was quite high, and Pam got out this small lawn mower. I was game for giving it a try.

She said she knew how to get it going. She yanked on the pull cord. Nothing happened. She yanked harder. Nothing happened. She yanked again and again. She couldn't get the engine to turn over. After a while, her face was beet red and she was sweating. She primed the carburetor, caught her breadth, and tried again. Finally, she gave up and told me to try.

Feeling my oats, I thought that I would have an easy time of it. I didn't. I could do no better than she did. I pulled so hard the mower would come off the ground. The pull cord was fraying. I was beet red and fatigued. Why in the world was it so hard to turn the engine over?

I never saw a lawn mower like it. I then began to use my noodle.

The pull cord turns the blade. The blade is sitting in the deep grass. To get the blade moving it has to rub against the deep grass. Feeling like a dummy I said, "I got it." I moved the mower onto the cement walk, gave it a yank, and Holla! It started! She gave me little credit for my flash of insight. Besides, the grass was so tall that the mower kept stalling out. I could cut only a small portion of it.

The Button Box

During the 1930's and 40's, my father bought 78rmp records of Bohemian music. This music was part of the home environment when I was very young. I remember it creating an atmosphere of home. Given my early age, I have only faint recollection of it. As recording technology changed, 78 rpm records became obsolete. In the 1950's, my father didn't buy records, and one by one, the old 78's were broken. They broke easily because they were made of brittle material, usually a shellac resin. The plastic records that succeeded them were advertised as unbreakable. My brother replaced our old phonograph with then current technology and bought his own music. The old Bohemian music was lost to me in the mists of childhood memory.

Most of my father's music wasn't reproduced in the new recording mediums—— dominantly, the LP record. My father moved onto my brother's tastes. All of this was good, but an emotional hole was left in me for the old music. I moved to rock and roll and then classical music.

While scavenging a Salvation Army store in the 1980's, I came upon some records that seemed to be of the sort I heard as a child. For many years I had found no such 78's in second-hand stores. I guessed that at this time the old timers who had these records were now dying off. Their possessions were being donated to charity.

I set out to hear some of this music. I wanted to encounter it again to see whether it jibed with my cloudy memories of a long-lost time. I began a serious search of second-hand stores near the old Czech neighborhoods. On each visit, there would be a new pile of 78rpm records that I would sort through. It didn't take long for the right material to show up. Then, more of it turned up.

I found few records pressed in Europe but quite a few produced in the U.S. Many recordings were from Cleveland during my father's era. A number were recorded by his boyhood friend Jerry Mazanec. I suspected that just as this kind of record appeared in the second-hand shops, it would disappear forever as the old timers' recordings were depleted.

I took my treasures home, washed them with dish soap to remove the dirt, and played them. Some were musical duds, others unfamiliar but too monotonous, but others were right on target. It took quite of bit of scavenging to come up with the right sort of material. In all, my searches yielded about 30 records that meant something to me. For example, my brother told me that I had found a recording that my father bought just before I was born. My father danced to it around the living room holding me in a blanket.

My grandfather, and then my brother played the button box accordion. It is called a "button box" for literal reasons. It has buttons in place of keys, and it is in the shape of a box. There are 34 buttons in the treble section for the right hand and eleven buttons in the bass for the left hand.

The accordion is a reed instrument, and the button box has a number of reeds that can melt your heart. It snorted in the bass. It made to-die-for chords in the lower register of the treble side. I decided to buy a button box, teach myself to play it, and pick out tunes that I heard on the 78's.

The trouble with learning to play the button box was that it wasn't organized like a piano keyboard with all the notes in sequence by pitch. The pitches jumped around and usually any two adjacent buttons would sound a chord. It had many fewer notes than a piano accordion. On the piano keyboard, there were white and black keys. The black keys were the sharps and flats. On my button box, there was only one flat—- B flat. This limited its repertoire, and it was a challenge and sometimes impossible to adapt the button box to what I heard on those scratchy 78 rpm records.

Most daunting was the feature that a button played a different note when you pulled the bellows out than when you pushed the bellows in. The short of it was that the button box was its own animal. After matching the notes to keys on my harpsichord in order to know its pitches, I set out to find the music of my childhood within it. I am up to more than a dozen tunes and still counting.

Minimum Requirement

As a teacher of philosophy in an urban community college, I was demanding of my students. I tried to help them catch up with their private college peers. I did a lot of writing on the chalkboard. One day I was writing on the board when this muffled animal sound came from the class. I paid it no mind. Then there was another somewhat different sound. I kept writing. At the third sound, I turned around. My blood was up. I thought that I would straighten out the wise guy. I looked around the room and saw no one that looked unusual. Then an oinking sound happened and the class began to laugh. I laughed too. There in the front row was a student sound asleep.

We continued to laugh with each new sound. The laughter finally caused him to stir. When he woke up, he did not know why we were laughing. I told him that it is one thing to sleep in class. That was not so bad, but that I had a strict no snoring rule. He later explained that he was on the wrestling team. He was exhausted from practice. He was starving from trying to make weight. I told him that I sympathized but no more snoring!

Philosophers like to use cute examples to illustrate their points. These are both conceits for us and colorful so that they stick in the student's mind. In talking about metaphysics, leprechauns are a favorite example. Part of the idea is to use a being that no one accepts as real. Unicorns are another favorite. Well, as I began to use leprechauns in my lecture, this elderly man in the class piped in, "You have to watch out for those leprechauns." I was cautious.

In looking at the student, I judged whether he was joking or was serious. I realized that he was serious. He went on, "Those leprechauns are going to get you." He also said something about the racetrack. The other students in the class had little patience for this sort of talk. Students told me after class that the student was an alcoholic and that they smelled alcohol on his breath. Perhaps leprechauns were real to him. On to Grinches as a lecture example?

The County Classroom

One of my major jobs at the college was to develop curriculum for a general education humanities program. My aspiration was to help students develop a love of the humanities. I regarded love of the humanities as more than being in the role of consumer and spectator. It was more than academic study of the arts. It involved participation in humanities institutions, interaction with humanists, and creative work of one's own. I believed that a life with the humanities was an important component of following Socrates' injunction to live an examined life. He taught that for us humans, the unexamined life is not worth living.

Cleveland is the center of Cuyahoga County. The county happens to be rich in humanities institutions—arts organizations, historical museums, colleges, and libraries. There are dozens of venues for the performing arts. My aim was to follow the lead of my colleague Ed Miggins in getting students out of the classroom and into the community. Ours was a commuter college. Most students had cars.

One of my course requirements was for students to present event reports of concerts, lectures, dance programs, theater productions, film screenings, and so on. At the start of each humanities class, some students would present reports. The reports usually set a positive tone and gave the class ideas about events they could attend. My aim was to open up the world of the humanities with resources that were readily available.

I had an advance man, Cliff Bendau, who visited museums, orchestras, theaters, and other colleges to introduce our program. They were receptive to Cliff and then our students because the humanities program was a way for them to build future audiences. We were flooded with their program literature.

I bought the largest road map of Cuyahoga County that I could find. I mounted it and hung it on a prominent wall of the college. I put pins in the map for where events were occurring then and into weekends. The pins were keyed to event literature posted beside the map. I eventually wanted to replace the pins with lights. That way, humanities students as well as the student body generally could see at a glance what was going on currently in the humanities. I provided enough information on the wall for them to plan a trip to an event.

The County In The Classroom

I also had the reverse aim to bring the community into the classroom. A large number of artists and humanists lived in Northern Ohio. Most of them lived nearby or were even neighbors.

During the first week of a course, I worked with students to choose creators in the arts to come speak to us and share their work. Students could pick a painter, poet, opera singer, or what have you. I would then draw on my lists of contacts to book them. Dozens of speakers shared their life's passions.

We had the great poet James C. Kilgore, the well-known sculptor Norman Poirer, the social activist Allen Bell, and the painter Kartek Trevedi. We had a music festival with The Mr. Stress Blues Band, the rock band Orville Normal, and the folk music duo of Jan Bogo and Peter Haskil. The experiences took the creative person off the pedestal and into personal interactions with our students. By George, they were interesting and friendly people that could be living down the street from us.

Through experiences with the visual and performing arts throughout the county and with artists and creative people visiting campus to interact with students, my hope was that students would become comfortable taking advantage of resources in their backyards. I hoped that resistance to try what is unfamiliar would be reduced. I found out that some students had spent their lives in the suburbs and were unfamiliar with the world-class arts institutions close by.

One gem of an institution is The Cleveland Museum of Art. It has always been free and open to the public. Once on a fieldtrip to the museum, most of the class went ahead in their cars, and I came a little later waiting for late-comers before leaving the college. When I arrived at the museum, I found my students standing along the wall in the lobby. I asked them why they weren't looking at art works. They said that they didn't know that they were allowed to just walk around! I never expected such a barrier. The average age of students at the college was 29.

Being Warped Toward Our Strengths

A rationale for my humanities program was inspired by how warped we became through twelve years of the standard grading system. I thought about how I was warped and how my peers were too. I set out to counteract it.

I thought that getting an excellent grade encouraged students to like and put effort toward what they were already good at or could quickly become good at. Lower grades discouraged students from liking and putting effort toward what they couldn't presently do well and had difficulty learning quickly.

Over the course of primary and secondary education, students often gravitated toward activities that showed their strengths. They shied away from activities that showed their weaknesses. This was because schooling was in a social environment. What others thought mattered greatly.

So, much of motivation was based in attitude. If someone was already beyond their peers in a subject area or skill, a good attitude emerged toward what came easy to them. Excellent grades and teacher praise came without great effort. The excellent grade provided incentive to pursue more of that subject.

The reverse also seemed true. If someone was behind their peers in a subject, they struggled to stay with the class. Little praise came their way, and often they were publicly identified as having difficulty. Excellent grades only came with great effort if at all. This struggle was a deterrent to putting forth effort to make up for weaknesses. The attitude of "I don't care," or "I don't even try" was used as a cover. For many students, weaknesses were carried from year to year often due to lack of interest and effort.

The result of twelve years of warped development toward strengths and away from weaknesses left many students on the threshold of adulthood with advanced abilities in some areas and hardly touched potentials in others.

But <u>what if</u> a student liked or identified with an activity but was not someone who showed great talent in it. Jump ahead to that person as an adult. They might want to give that activity a go-around. They might suspect that they would like it, enjoy it, and find it fulfilling.

So, my aim in the humanities courses was for students to identify activities that they found alluring that were part of their unfulfilled potential. I told students that with just one humanities course, they shouldn't expect to make up for a life-time of being warped. However, they should expect to have a positive experience. They should expect to make significant strides. I tried to reverse the negative work of the grading system.

Suppose a student through their twelve years of schooling had become an excellent dancer. It would require great effort to become just a little bit better. If an average adult can hardly dance, a little effort can often show important progress. Initial steps in an activity are often big ones.

So, I wanted students to engage in affirming activities that I hoped were life-changing. In the best case, I would help a student develop an enduring interest in a humanities activity. From my point of view, what students were motivated to do after the course was over was more important than cramming information for tests. Moreover, students who affirmed an activity might further their interest at the college. Our program could be a feeder for traditional subject areas.

Humanities Projects

The key to unlocking student potential was the humanities project. A student had to complete a major project for each course. The last days of a term were devoted to students presenting their projects to the class. I encouraged students to do a project on some art or humanity that they thought about doing some day but put off. The ideal aim was to further an interest toward something that they felt tentative about—-something they never quite got around to.

Since I was asking students to take risks and maybe expose their inabilities to the class, I was not demanding about project topics in the beginning. I also did not want grades to stand in the way of risk taking. So, I assured students that they would earn an A or B if they had a project and presented it to the class. Most projects were heart felt.

Students learned to trust the group and many of them blossomed. Most students in a class were also very encouraging to students who said they took a risk and exposed their inabilities. The end of a term was a variety show that students looked forward to.

Students with some experience working in the arts took off with creative projects. We had student poets, painters, singers, thinkers, and so on. We had group projects like play readings, multi-media performances, and dance demonstrations. Students formed groups outside of class and invited me to dip in and out of their creative process.

As the number of sections of the courses mushroomed, I hired several part-time teachers. Most of them felt humbled and even threatened by the process. No one had a background in enough of the humanities to claim general competence. I told them that I felt the same way. I regarded my students as younger colleagues. In my sections of courses, I designated myself "the course friend" rather than professor. I was more a facilitator than a teacher. I learned much from my students.

The Problem of Too Much Comfort

A down side of my humanities course design was that a very few students were too comfortable with the easy rules. They took the guarantee of a good grade to let them off the hook. Some of these cases were hilarious, others tragic, and others yet pathetic.

One student said that he tried to learn to be a ventriloquist. He brought in a regular ventriloquist's dummy. He put it on his lap.

Everything the dummy was supposed to say, the student said while moving his lips in the normal way. There was no ventriloquism! As he started to do this, the class roared. It was a great comedy routine. He had to rehearse it to get his timing down. How well did his project meet course expectations?

The writer Paul Goodman said that what everyone learned in high school was how to get by. In seventh grade wood shop, students in the Cleveland Public Schools had the same projects to complete. One of them was a pump lamp — a lamp base in the shape of a water pump. You pumped the handle to turn the lamp on. In thousands of homes in the Cleveland area, parents still had their son's pump lamp on display. I recognized one of my humanities students from my days in junior high school. He did not recognize me. For his humanities project, he turned in a pump lamp! When I saw it I said, "Oh my god, a Cleveland Public Schools pump lamp."

The strangest case was a student who enjoyed being in the class. He enjoyed hobnobbing with others in discussion groups. He was likable and personable. He acted like a gracious and motivated student. At the end of the term, he alerted me to the fact that he was having trouble coming up with a project topic. I made some suggestions. The day of his presentation arrived. He said to the class that he was walking by a bookstore in downtown Cleveland and saw a humanities book. He thought that humanities students at the college would benefit from reading it. As his project, he donated it to the library! He inscribed a message indicating his generosity, signed and dated it.

Educational Pragmatism

With the humanities courses, I adopted the stance of our campus president Robert Shepack. To him, every educational effort was an experiment. You used the results of each experiment to modify teaching practice. The theory was that instruction and thereby student learning will improve step by step. I learned, however, that teaching practice is constrained by its context. For example, teaching practice can't outpace administrative will and budgetary constraints. That is where I had some problems.

The humanities courses were an outstanding success in enrollment. They were very popular with students. In order to continue developing the courses I applied what I was learning term by term. I was discovering that many of the obstacles and problems I encountered could be directly addressed through individualized instruction. This implied smaller class sizes.

I discovered that students would develop further on their projects from in-class work. This required having a humanities lab. The lab would not be expensive. We needed running water and a few supplies. It did require a dedicated space. Shepack was unwilling to dedicate space. He was unwilling to reduce class sizes of humanities courses. We continued with large-group instruction.

In the end, whether students developed lifelong interests in the humanities remains an unknown. As with most teaching, you never know what effect you have on the future quality of a student's life. I hoped that student efforts had effects in the direction I intended. I think that my eclectic approach to the humanities aimed for worthy goals.

You could say that the rest of my teaching career in philosophy and the humanities was history or that I lived "Happily Ever After." But sixty to seventy hours per week, year after year was wearing. I had quickly reached the limits of what the administration was willing to support. I also learned how far I could press my students for achievement. I faced how far I could go in breaking with tradition. Nevertheless, I had many joyous years in the classroom. I saw a large number of my students come of age in taking themselves and their education seriously.

No Perishing

In teaching at a community college, I didn't have the job requirement of publishing. I wasn't under the "publish or perish" imperative. I preferred it that way. I was a teacher and that's where I wanted to put my effort. I wanted to design curriculum, work on my presentations, and interact with students. I did want to write philosophy, but on my terms.

I didn't want to spend my career pleasing editors of journals and book publishers. I didn't want the pressure of publishing on deadlines. I didn't want to settle for doing publishable work that was only a minor extension of the literature. I think I could have been successful "playing the professional game," but I think I would have produced little that was deeply satisfying to me and little that was more than a footnote to the vast then-current literature.

I realized during my graduate education that the work of extending the literature in certain directions would get done without me. There were thousands of philosophers diligently performing this task. My talents weren't needed. At the community college, I had the freedom to work at my own pace, pursuing what interested me, that called for my talents in particular.

Fame, fortune, and recognition always seemed elusive targets, that even if achieved, would be fleeting and by and large for the wrong reasons. I told myself that philosophy well done is written for the long haul, not for the here and now. This is not to say that I thought I had the talent, insight, or creative ability to write enduring work. I always thought it was worthwhile to do my best. To do that, I had to take my time.

You may think that my sort of thinking was too easy, in effect, to stay out of the competition. To let people of a later time and place decide whether my efforts mattered in the end. I didn't take it as a cop-out because I didn't need competition to be motivated.

Doing work is separate from how well the world receives it. I took a lesson from many others who led obscure lives but did a significant amount of work. I granted that our time was different. It offered myriad opportunities for promotion of work as well as self-promotion. Shouldn't I have taken advantage of them? Under most circumstances, I told myself, promotion and marketing shouldn't be major life activities. Time and effort spent in marketing blurs into the chances of achieving the greater ends of life. Living well and doing well mattered more.

Filling Gaps

So, how did my writing go? The answer covers ground beyond my middle life, but if you stayed with this book this far, you probably are curious how my writing ended up.

Since my time for writing was more limited than my university colleagues, I was very fussy what I decided to write about. I would take up many projects during the summers when I didn't have to teach. I usually chose topics that in my estimation others would not write about. A topic had to interest me, be something about which I think I had something to say, that would be important to philosophy in a broader context.

Needless to say, much of my output did not strike a chord with journal editors or referees for conferences. I also discovered that there was a bias within the profession against community college philosophers. My attitude was and still is that I wasn't writing for official gatekeepers or to please them. I was writing to advance the field—-fill what I took to be important gaps.

Minor journals and societies liked my work and most of it found its way into print. Some of it initiated discussions of neglected topics. A sampling includes papers on appreciation, wilderness experience, negative empathy, the ethics of being educated, the difference between art and the world, and human obsolescence. I also wrote several books including textbooks, a book on the human future, and a novel.

My wife Kathy is a nurse researcher and pioneered the theory of comfort in nursing. She has an influential website The Comfortline, and she developed an international following of researchers. We co-authored a number of papers. I worked on the philosophical end and she worked on the nursing research and theory end. She has an impressive array of research papers. All in all, I think her work has been applied to do much human good.

So, I have been fortunate. I was able to integrate my livelihood with my interests, use my talents, and produce creative work that, in my opinion, needed to be done. It could be argued that in important ways I should have paid greater attention to the wider world. Perhaps

I should have, but I have the gnawing suspicion, that direction would have led to regrets. We live in a society where individualism is a credo but group conformity is the norm. Conformity is within a mass society where most of us remain anonymous anyway. In the end, individual wellbeing depends more upon what we do than what we say or even aspire to.

The Refrigerator Heater

It was a mighty cold winter. Biting wind, below zero, and much snow. I was staying with colleague Ed Miggins and his wife Janet for a few days before continuing my sabbatical leave at The University of Wisconsin. Janet was into saving money on utilities. They had a large old house with high ceilings and leaky windows. She warned me that she turns the thermostat way down at night. I went to bed fully dressed for the next day. I also had thick covers.

In the morning, the house was so cold that it was hard to get used to. I touched the radiators. No warmth there. I went down stairs to assemble breakfast. I got the cereal box and a banana. I went to the refrigerator to get milk. I put my hand in and it seemed odd. I then realized that the refrigerator was warm. The refrigerator was warmer than the house! I joked with Janet that she should come down stairs in the morning and open the refrigerator door to warm the kitchen for the rest of us.

The Wolf Spider

I had moved to a cottage near several square miles of woods. It was peaceful and full of natural sounds. During the summer, I got in the habit of sleeping late. I knew that I shouldn't sleep late because when I would wake up, I would feel half-baked. I liked comfortable slippers. The sort that was most comfortable were the cheap ones. They were always nearly falling apart. They looked terrible, but Ah! they were comfortable. As I got out of bed one late morning, groggy, and half asleep, I slid into my slippers and began to lift my right foot to head to the kitchen. I noticed that there was something in the toe. It felt like a piece of rubber. This often happened where some rubber from inside the slipper would break off. I wiggled my toes trying to move the rubber out of my step. It wasn't working.

I took off the slipper to shake out the rubber. Lo and behold, on the floor in front of me was this hairy brown and white spider the size of a portabella mushroom. Well, not quite that big, but almost! As Woody Allen said in the movie *Annie Hall*, "Major spider." What was it doing out of the circus? I did a double take. I woke up fast. My heart was pounding. I took a large frying pan from the kitchen to do battle with it. Even an hour later, I went back to look at the carcass. Yup, it was that big. Yoooo! I asked a biology teacher at school about what kind of spider it might be. She said that it was probably a wolf spider. She also said that it didn't escape from the circus and added that our friends the wolf spiders walk among us.

Slithering

The entrance to the cottage was at ground level. You first entered the utility room, passed the furnace, and then you took a step up to the door to the main living area. One night when returning home, I unlocked the door and reached in to turn on the ceiling light. As the light went on, I caught a glimpse of the tail of a snake disappearing behind the furnace. That tail whipping behind the furnace was enough to get my heart pounding. It came in with me. It "must" have been waiting for me by the door. As I opened the door, it snuck in. I thought, "This does not look good."

I quietly went over to the furnace. I grabbed the furnace, went up on tiptoes, and peered down at the snake. Whoa! Big snake. It was about three feet long! How am I going to get the big fella out of there? I got a weapon —a broom. I swept forward and said, "Shoo snake! Shoo." By the sound that it made, it was not happy. It stared at me with those beady eyes. I looked right back. I wasn't happy either. I couldn't grab it; it being down behind the furnace. I got a cup of water and poured a little on it. The snake darted beneath a chest. I guess it was not a water snake.

I lifted the chest with one hand, aimed my broom and let the snake have it. The darned thing went back behind the furnace. By this time, I was getting worked up. I opened the door, and put the chest outside. I left no place for it to hide. I wet the snake again, shooed it to door with my broom. It finally had the good sense to leave.

Ansel's Cave

A few-mile hike in the woods behind the cottage led to an area where Ansel's Cave was supposed to be. Legend had it that Ansel Savage was the first resident in the Russell Township area in the early nineteenth century. He lived in the cave and started a business as a cobbler. He was the earliest politician in the township. The first politician? A caveman? Sounds right. After Ansel left the cave for better digs, counterfeiters were supposed to have occupied it. No one was quite sure where the cave was. My lady friend Kathy and I set out to find it.

In these woods, the terrain under the forest canopy was all chopped up. This happened during the ice age. There were many creeks, exposed rock outcroppings, waterfalls, and ravines. Each time, we spent an hour hiking to the area. We had a little time to explore for the cave. We then had an hour hike back to the cottage. The search made for many interesting hikes. Once we found a newborn fawn. Another time a bald eagle was menacing us. Another time we walked through ground cover that had purple pollen. We kicked up clouds of pollen walking through it.

We came upon an area that could have been the cave. It had thirty-foot walls. It was large enough to set up living quarters in. The only problem was that it would flood whenever the dry stream bed would fill with runoff. Some locals thought that the cave was destroyed by the highway that crossed the area. Others thought that the area we found was the cave. We searched for counterfeiting gear or bad coins. We found none.

Real Chicken Soup

When Kathy and I were newlyweds, we had many conversations about things that we liked. She by and large knew what I liked in the way of food. When she brought up the question about food again, I thought long and hard about what was missing. I remembered that my mother made this delicious chicken soup way back in the nineteen fifties. It tasted like chicken. It tasted like chicken more so than any chicken soup I had had since. It had fresh parsley in it. Noodles were home-made egg noodles. I asked Mom for the recipe.

My mother mentioned the recipe but acted like the soup was not special. It was a basic recipe. Boil a chicken. Pick the parsley from the garden. Make the noodles. Put them in the pot. I told Mom that the soup was the best I ever tasted and that there had to be more to it than that. She said that you needed a stewing chicken. Kathy and I searched far and wide for a stewing chicken. Food markets don't carry them and can't order them. We went to the big public market on Cleveland's near west side. None of the vendors could come up with a stewing chicken either. We settled for the next best thing — a roaster.

We made the soup. It was disappointing. It was thin. It lacked flavor. It did not have the right color. We went back to Mom. She said that you needed an old, tough, stringy chicken. She said that the soup will be wonderful but the boiled meat will be bland and difficult to chew. Come to think of it, I remember the soup as the best part of the meal. After the soup, we had the boiled meat. It was tough and stringy. It was rather tasteless. I then asked Mom why she didn't make the wonderful soup after the nineteen fifties. She said that it was too much work.

What work was there? She said that it was much easier to buy dried noodles in a bag. They were cheap. She usually had some parsley in the garden, but if there wasn't, parsley was also cheap. After the neighborhood butcher shops closed, you could not get a real stewing chicken. Then she said that she did not remember the soup being that special. It was good but not wonderful. I asked her why she thought that.

It turns out that my mother made the soup while my dad was out on strike from the steel mill. We had little money to live on. Mom tried to economize. She bought the cheapest chicken — an old tough bird that few would buy. She made noodles the hard and inexpensive way. She mixed the dough, rolled it out, and cut noodles with a knife. She used garden parsley. The soup brought back memories of hard times. During those hard times, she certainly protected me from her worries. I only remembered the soup!

A Delicate Breeze on my Face

After Kathy and I were married, I joined Kathy and my three step-daughters, Chris, Jill, and Liz, in a historic brick farm-house close to our village's downtown. In 1865 when the house was built, small farms were where residential streets are now. We were in the dog days of August, hot and humid. The house didn't have air-conditioning. For most of the summer, we didn't need it since giant shade trees blocked direct sun most of the day. At night, we kept the windows open, and we had a ceiling fan to circulate the air.

About a week into being married, we were two days into a heat wave. We turned out the lights and were about to go to sleep. It was very quiet so a little rustling became noticeable. I felt a tiny rush of air on my cheek. Wff, wff, wff. I rolled over. It happened again. Wff, wff. I poked Kathy and said, "I think there is something in the room." She said I was imagining things and to go to sleep. I settled back in. Then I heard more rustling and more whiffing on my cheek. I started and said, "Something is in the room. I feel its breath. Turn on the light."

The lamp was on Kathy's side of the bed. She turned on the light. Whoa! There was a bat circling the bed. My heart began to beat very fast. Kathy had this worried look. What were we to do? Well, since we were now fully awake and we had to get the bat out of the house, I went for a broom. She went for a waste basket. The plan was that I would swat it with the broom and she would quickly put the inverted basket over it while it was stunned on the floor. I swung once. I swung twice. I kept missing the bat. It was sort of like a cartoon. I swung every which way and I kept missing the bat. It then occurred to me that a bat's sonar enabled it to dodge the broom. I sent Kathy for reinforcements—- a second broom.

In excited tone, I told Kathy to swing at the bat, and then, I would swing right after. The idea was that as the bat made an evasive maneuver, I would clobber it. We did swing a couple of times. It finally worked. There it was trying to recover on the floor. We put the waste basket over it pushing its wing a bit to get it all under the basket. What would we do then? We needed a cover. We took a clip board and slid it under the basket. The bat was now captured. We opened the window screen, went to the window with the basket, and shooed it into the night.

We had more bat problems, but now we knew what to do. Feeling the air on my cheek off the wings of a bat still gave me the chills. Euw! If you tell me that bats are our friends, I will agree. But I like bats in their place. They should not be hovering so close to my face that I feel a breeze from their wings. We knew also that some bats carried rabies.

That summer some neighbors and friends had bat problems too. They would call us. We would come over with our two brooms and waste basket with clip board. My heart still pounded hard when capturing a bat. I didn't get used to doing it.

I tried to seal up the house. The bats were getting in somewhere. I plugged holes in the foundation. Looked under the eaves. Checked cracks in window framing. Still, when it was hot and humid another bat would appear. Just as I thought I had solved the bat-problem, my optimism would be shattered. We would be watching TV in the family room when we would catch a glimpse, from the corner of our eyes, of a shadow ducking and darting in the kitchen.

We had a guy service our forced-air furnace. I asked him about bats. How could they get in? He offered the following explanation. When it is hot and humid, bats sleep on cooler masonry like in chimneys. Cool air from the basement gets trapped there by the thick humid air above. A furnace has a gas pilot light. The exhaust gasses from the pilot collect in the chimney. The bats sleeping on the chimney walls become drowsy and fall to the bottom.

As they recover, they crawl up the chimney toward a breeze coming from the vent pipe linking the furnace to the chimney. They crawl down the vent pipe. They reach the air intake for the vent that causes the air to flow up the chimney. They fall to the floor of the basement. Once in the house, they make their way to the upstairs rooms. They make this journey stealthily and at night. All the while they are trying to find a way to escape from the house.

Since they are nocturnal, they hide in wait in a bedroom for the lights to be turned out. That is the time they come to life and seek out sleepers. The bat thinks, "That guy looks promising. I'll go hover over <u>his</u> face!" There you have it.

Crab Carcass and the Turtle Patrol

Several years after being married, Kathy and I were able to vacation with Chris, Jill, Liz and their families at Kiawah Island beach in South Carolina. I had taken up running and one morning while on a run up the beach, I had a chance encounter with Lowell Bernard. He was a neighbor from our town. He retired from being the director of The Cleveland Health Museum and moved to South Carolina. He and his wife Diana were looking at loggerhead turtle nests. They were volunteers for The Turtle Patrol a group that worked on conserving the loggerhead turtles that nested on the beach. Lowell invited our family to help unpack a turtle nest the next morning.

During my run down the beach, I passed a dead horseshoe crab that was pretty well intact. In South Carolina, adult horseshoe crabs are about two feet from tail to the crest of the shell and a foot wide. This one was up to that standard. I decided to pick it up on my way back to our umbrellas. I was going to run while carrying it. When I lifted the thing, it was heavy with water and stunk to high heaven. I could hardly run while lugging that thing.

As I approached our umbrellas and the family, I was worn out. Breathing hard and red in the face, I proudly held up the crab carcass for all to admire. But as I got closer, I heard, "Peee-U! Why would you want that thing? What are you going to do with it?" I replied, "It's a trophy." They replied, "It stinks! Get rid of it." Crestfallen but not dis-couraged, I took it back to our condo, cleaned it as best I could, and left it on an upper porch.

When I found it, it was rotting and when I put it on the porch it became full of maggots. As days wore on, it smelled worse with many flies emerging from it. While all of this was going on, the family kept encouraging me to throw it away. "What are you going to do with that thing? We're not going to take it in the car." Well, I had flown down because of my summer teaching schedule. I said, "Don't worry, I will take it on the plane."

Grandchildren, Ted, Meg, and Cate were willing to get up at 5 in the morning to see what The Turtle Patrol was all about. As dawn broke, Kathy and I, our daughter Jill, and the grandkids met Lowell, Diana, and the rest of the patrol. When they unpacked the nest, there were quite a few eggs that had hatched.

The little turtles were autotropic. They would walk toward the sun, and the sun was rising near the distant shoreline to our far left. From where we were, this was not in a straight line to the ocean. If nature took its course, the turtles would walk toward the sun quite a way down the beach before they entered the water.

One role of the turtle patrol was to escort turtles to the water. You stood over a turtle blocking the sun and with your feet, you presented an obstacle that directed the turtle in a straight line to the water. Ted and Meg, being older than Cate, jumped right into this activity. We were told that the turtles imprint this journey. The mature females return to this beach and follow the same path to lay their eggs.

A related role was to protect the turtles at a perilous time in their lives. The longer a turtle stayed on the beach, the longer it was vulner-able to predators. The main predators at this time of day were gulls and ghost crabs. The crabs would blind the baby turtles. The result was that the turtles would walk in circles until eaten by the crabs. The Turtle Patrol prevented the crabs and gulls from getting to the turtles.

When the fragile little loggerheads would reach the surf, the waves would crash over them and sweep them back to the beach. They would try again and again until they were able to enter the water. As they swam away, there was a great sense of satisfaction. The grandkids will never forget their experience working to save the turtles.

After the maggots hatched, the crab carcass didn't smell as bad. All of the rot was gone. But it didn't smell so good either. I packed it in plastic grocery bags and sealed it up. I carried it on the plane and put it in the overhead bin. I didn't notice any foul odors. Honest, I didn't.

The big horseshoe crabs off the coast of South Carolina had black shells. I washed my shell, and as I expected, it was still black. I decided to urethane it. The varnish transformed it. Unusual features and patterns were revealed. Overall, it was an enormously ancient-looking animal. The shell had a gray/beige/green glazed masonry look to it. It was like stain bringing out features on a lab-slide. It hangs on the wall of my study.

One Thing at a Time

Like so many before me, I was inspired by the ideal of the Renaissance Man. The ideal was Leonardo da Vinci or even Enlightenment personages like Thomas Jefferson or Mary Wollstonecraft. The tragedy of human life was that our expansive genetic potential had too few years to play itself out. We would all die unfulfilled. The Renaissance Individual came closest to realizing their potential. The different dimensions of their personality were realized in creative activities.

Over the years, I tried to do a number of creative activities. I found out that when I put a full effort into my teaching, I had little energy left for playing music. It was hard to concentrate that many hours. My emotional energy was by and large spent. If I put a full measure into playing music, my writing would suffer. If my writing was coming along, I would be on edge and my teaching would suffer. Experience taught me that I could only do well in one fully engaging activity at a time. Maybe the Renaissance Man had a way to integrate a number of fully engaging activities into one super activity. I just don't know.

Following Your Nose

Throughout my adult life, I thought that life would be best when we follow our natural inclinations like a dog following its nose through the forest. Dogs sleep a lot. They yawn a bit. They are often bored. They sniff a lot, but soon they realize that nothing interesting has turned up. Kathy and I had a basset hound named Archie. When we would take him to the woods, it would be a wholly different picture. Archie would follow his nose. He would run here and there. He would be alert and fully involved but yet relaxed in a peaceful way. Archie's behavior expressed the fulfillment of his endowment as it was fully integrated with the environment. Following his nose was what that dog did best.

When we would decide that the run was over, we would call to him. "Here Archie!" He would run on pretending not to hear. As we would call again, Archie slowed down a bit but still pretended not to hear. We yelled louder, "Archie come here right now!" He would slowly come to us. The outing was over. Archie reverted to his domesticated behavior. The elegant integration of dog with environment had ended.

A challenge for we humans is, "How can we be like the dog following our noses?" What would a human life be like where we were elegant and integrated with our environment? The fulfillment of which of our natural inclinations would make this happen? In trying to answer these questions for myself, I determined that the activity would need to be disciplined while not rigidly disciplining ourselves. When we disciplined ourselves, we forced ourselves to do things. We were not following our inclinations.

When we perform disciplined activities, like dance, sports, writing, our energy is channeled in a very precise way, like the dog's. We need discipline to get good at those activities through practice. Once we are good at them, we could perform in a natural way using what we had learned. Archie was guided by his senses. We seem to be able to select a wide range of activities and make them look natural. Sometimes I felt that I was doing creative activities in a way that was like Archie following his nose. Most of the time, however, I didn't feel that way.

For years the dog analogy haunted me. Was I hopelessly

domesticated? Do I have other natural instincts to tap into? Would they involve limited activities, like the dog's, such as chasing down game or hunting? Is human life much more complicated and harder to manage? Did our lives become helplessly unnatural with industrialization? I am still seeking answers.

Post Script

Life goes on with all of its fulfillments, distractions, and problems. Much experience is hum drum. Hard experience continues as well. Life in the long run offers a spectrum of challenges. I find it easy to slip into a serious or even dark mood. My aim in these pages, however, was to tell some of my story through lighter moments from the thicket of personal history. Even so, my stories often have a dark angle. At places you might have said to yourself, "That is not funny." I probably would agree if I shared your perspective.

Charm and humor depend on a person's disposition to them. I hope that for the most part, I struck a charm button or tickled your humor bone. In everyday living, I am often caught off guard by tales coming to life again, popping out of memory. They are like lost gems sparkling brilliantly on the beach of my early and middle life.

CPSIA information can be obtained
at www.ICGtesting.com
Printed in the USA
FSHW020914180521
81464FS

9 781977 239983